The Food & Feelings Workbook

A Full Course Meal on Emotional Health

Karen R. Koenig, LCSW, M.Ed

The Food & Feelings Workbook
A Full Course Meal on Emotional Health

Gürze Books
P.O. Box 2238
Carlsbad, CA 92018
760-434-7533
www.gurze.com

Cover design by Johnson Design
www.bookjacketdesign.com

Author photo by Sue Messina
www.suemessinaphotography.com

Library of Congress Cataloging-in-Publication Data

Koenig, Karen R., 1947-
The food & feelings workbook : a full course meal on emotional health / Karen R. Koenig.
p. cm.
ISBN-13: 978-0-936077-20-8
ISBN-10: 0-936077-20-4
1. Eating disorders--Prevention. 2. Food--Psychological aspects. 3. Food habits--Psychological aspects. I. Title.
II. Title: Food and feelings workbook.
RC552.E18K63 2007
616.85'26--dc22

2006100432

NOTE:
The author and publisher of this book intend for this publication to provide accurate information. It is sold with the understanding that it is meant to complement, not substitute for, professional medical and/or psychological services.

59086

To my husband, Keith—many thanks yet again.

Contents

Acknowledgments

Over the decades I've counseled and taught hundreds of troubled eaters and every one of them deserves a heartfelt thank you. As they poured their hearts out, kept digging away to discover what made them so crazy around food, and hunkered down for the hard work of overcoming their eating problems, I learned not just how tenacious an eating disorder can be, but also how resilient and courageous the human spirit is. I knew more than a bit about food and feelings from my own decades of self-destructive eating, but these wounded eaters rounded out my knowledge and helped me make connections I hadn't made before. To be honest, they taught me about as much as I taught them.

Gürze Books was right behind me from the get-go when I mentioned the idea of a book about food and feelings, and they remain terrific collaborators. Special thanks and indebtedness go to Lindsey Hall Cohn and Lindsay Woolman for the outstanding job they did reshaping my ideas and words into more readable form, and doing it all with such good humor and high enthusiasm. This workbook truly has been a team effort. Janice M. Pieroni, Esq., my agent, is a friend and never puts down her megaphone if it means missing an opportunity to cheer me on. Cheers back to her.

Introduction

In nearly thirty years of teaching and counseling, I've met scores of individuals who've impressed me with their incredible courage, doggedness, and passionate desire to heal their relationship with food. They generally ended up on my doorstep after decades of food and weight obsession, crash diets, binge eating, or food deprivation, shamefully aware of their distress and hoping against hope that I had an alternative to offer. As we talked and I explained the Cognitive-Behavioral treatment model I use—that our beliefs create our feelings and our feelings produce our behaviors, insight flickered in their eyes as they realized that there was more to change than just their eating habits.

Through our work together, these intrepid souls made tremendous changes in their thinking about eating, weight and body image as they moved toward developing a healthy belief system. They gradually relaxed around food as they followed the guidelines in my first book, *The Rules of "Normal" Eating*— 1) eating when you're hungry or have a particular craving, 2) selecting satisfying foods, 3) staying aware and focused on eating to maximize enjoyment, and 4) stopping when you're full or satisfied. With diligence and practice, they reduced their preoccupation with "good" and "bad" foods, increased their comfort dining with others, decreased their food binges, threw out their scales, started to find food pleasurable, and began to make peace with their bodies. For the first time in a long time (or maybe ever) they felt hopeful about resolving their food problems.

However, as time went on, I noticed a clear pattern: No matter how much their beliefs and behaviors changed, they remained stuck in one main area: handling their emotions. The same theme arose repeatedly—certain kinds of distress were too scary, overwhelming, anxiety-provoking, intense, and unbearable. They feared that allowing their discomfort to break into consciousness would overwhelm them and plunge them down a deep well of depression from which they'd never climb out. What if they went crazy and couldn't function? What if people stopped loving them because they weren't upbeat and uncomplaining? It was easier and felt safer to focus on preparing for another binge, skipping their next meal, or losing that last ten pounds than to face internal turmoil.

These individuals had a lesson to learn about emotional suffering: that feelings have intrinsic purpose and value and that each of them could fully and deeply be with their heart's pain without fracturing into a thousand tiny pieces. They needed to learn that *success in overcoming eating problems is directly related to experiencing a full range of emotions.* Not surprisingly, as I helped students and clients explore their feelings and fears about them, they became emotionally unstuck: They raged, whimpered, howled, and quivered; they dug up the past and eventually laid it to rest. They looked reality squarely in the eye and started to use their feelings to take care of themselves more effectively.

They also stood up for themselves and said "No" more often. They became appropriately selfish and acted as if they deserved good things in life. Feeling entitled to their emotions, they were able to grieve their losses and celebrate their joys and satisfactions. They also began to articulate what they wanted out of life, stopped taking care of everyone else's needs instead of their own, and moved toward nourishing themselves physically, mentally, emotionally, and spiritually.

Then, something else amazing happened: their eating problems gradually subsided. *Feeling* replaced focusing on food and weight.

The Food & Feelings Workbook has two goals. The first is to give you support in letting go of dysfunctional eating behaviors and the second is to help you create a happier, more satisfying life. Achieving both of these goals depends on learning to handle your emotions effectively and appropriately. And although all feelings are important, I chose to examine seven specific ones that are more likely than others to drive disordered eating: guilt, shame, helplessness, anxiety, disappointment, confusion, and loneliness. *Getting comfortable with these seven emotions is the only way to end a food and weight obsession once and for all.* By making a practice of acknowledging, identifying, experiencing, understanding, and following them, you'll be able to stop using food-related behaviors to regulate them. You'll learn to satisfy your deepest emotional longings appropriately and effectively, and as a result, your eating and your life will be transformed.

Our time on earth can feel far too long when we're overwhelmed with shame about eating, plagued by lack of self-trust, and believe we'll never learn the secrets to true happiness. But it's way too short when we're joyfully engaged in meaningful work, in nurturing, intimate relationships and when we love ourselves and get a charge out of being alive.

If you missed Emotions 101 the first time around, you're a member of a very large club. The good news is that, as an adult, you can learn all you need to know.

The Food & Feelings Workbook will teach you how to:

- welcome rather than fear feelings
- value feelings as a barometer and mediator between internal needs and external circumstance
- know when you have a feeling
- identify exactly what you're feeling
- bear feelings that you believe are intolerable
- use upsetting feelings to learn about your emotional needs
- take responsibility for all of your feelings

- handle your feelings appropriately and effectively
- use your feelings to improve your life and bring you happiness and satisfaction
- disconnect food from feeling and stop emotional food binges
- stop obsessing about food and weight
- stop using control of your food intake to distract yourself from feeling
- enjoy food as a delicious, sensory delight
- take care of yourself emotionally without focusing on food

At the beginning of this workbook, you'll find a *Food & Feelings Pre-Assessment* and at the end, a *Food & Feelings Post-Assessment.* Neither one reflects your intelligence or whether you're a good or bad person. Nor are they the final word on how you're doing with emotions or with food. Like feelings, these assessments are meant to provide you with tools to improve your life. They'll also show you how much you've grown by reading and using this workbook. Additionally, the *Post-Assessment* will point you toward specific areas that need more attention.

There are three types of exercises in each chapter: *Stop and Feel* questions, *Practice Exercises,* and questions for *Further Exploration.* Where indicated, be sure to write down your answers. My purpose in "forcing" you to put pen to paper is to nudge you out of your comfort zone. If there's no discomfort, there's no reason to change! The act of writing will also help you stay present and grounded. If you avoid these exercises or pass on answering in writing, you're running away from your feelings (no matter what excuses you give yourself). Think of me as pushing you to do something you know deep in your heart will be beneficial and worthwhile.

Stop and Feel Questions

Stop and Feel questions, which are sprinkled throughout the text, encourage you to discover and precisely label what you're experiencing in the moment about what you're reading. Each time you get to a *Stop and Feel,* please: 1) find a relaxing position that you can hold comfortably for a few minutes, 2) read the question slowly, 3) close your eyes, 4) wait for a response to surface within you, and 5) write down your reaction. You might capture a feeling immediately, have to wait for one to bubble up, or even find that you're experiencing more than one emotion. Just keep letting your feelings deepen and try not to cut off the exercise too quickly.

If you become impatient or frustrated that you don't feel anything or can't find an exact label for what you're experiencing, don't fret—frustration, impatience, confusion, and uncertainty are feelings too! Trust in the process until a response floats or pops into your consciousness. My hunch is that you might have trouble accessing your emotions the first few times you try, but that, with practice, they'll come more quickly and fluidly.

Searching for a response, you'll learn and practice two important skills: tuning in to authentic feelings, and identifying them correctly. So please, try to avoid plucking a response out of thin air—what you wish you felt or think you should feel. Simply connect to your heart without judgment—*Gee, I'm kind of curious but also a little frightened.* If you can't put your finger on a reaction within three minutes, just note this fact without defining yourself as bad, wrong or a failure, and return to wherever you left off reading. If boredom or anger is what's up for you, note that too, but make no judgment.

Additionally, focus on identifying a *feeling*, not a *thinking*, response—one from your heart, not from your head. People who aren't used to connecting with emotions frequently answer with *thinking* responses, such as when I ask a client who's recently lost a loved one how she's feeling and she says, "I'm doing okay," or "Everybody loses someone sometime." Thinking is a cognitive process; feeling is a more instinctive, gut reaction.

Here's an example of a *Stop and Feel* question:

✓ STOP AND FEEL

What are you feeling right now?

I'm afraid I'll have to give up focusing on food as a crutch, but I'm also excited about finally learning to make peace with eating and my body.

Practice Exercises

Practice Exercises, also scattered throughout the text, ask you to engage in specific behaviors and perform certain tasks that will give you a chance to put into action what you've been learning. Some are focused strictly on emotions, while others involve eating behaviors, and still others target both. These exercises will boost your proficiency in understanding and handling emotions and move you toward "normal eating." You can practice them over and over.

Once again, I expect and hope that these exercises will make you at least mildly uncomfortable because you'll be trying on new, unfamiliar behaviors. Never fear. With practice, you'll soon be able to take them on the road. It doesn't matter if they seem artificial, awkward, unsettling, and scary at first, which they most likely will. Do them enough and they can't help but become second nature.

Here's an example of a *Practice Exercise*. Give it a try! Remember, the more you practice, the more skilled you'll become.

☼ PRACTICE EXERCISE

Divining

PURPOSE: To divine whether you're hungry for food or are experiencing an emotion. As a water diviner is said to tune in to underground water with a divining rod, you're going to use your hand as tools for discovery.

WHAT YOU NEED: chair

DIRECTIONS: Have a seat and visualize a food that you think of as "forbidden" or that you have trouble resisting. At the same time, place one hand over your heart and one over your stomach.

Stay with the food image until you feel an internal stirring, a *something*. Now ask yourself: Do I feel a hunger in my stomach or a feeling in my heart—perhaps longing, sadness, or anxiety?

REFLECTION (to be done after completion of exercise): What did you feel when you visualized your "forbidden" food? Did you have a mix of reactions? Perhaps you learned that this food makes you long for the good old days when it comforted you in childhood or that it upsets you because you want it so badly, never eat it, or can't stop once you've started.

____

____

____

Further Exploration

At the end of each chapter, you'll find questions for *Further Exploration* along with space for written responses. These are meant to help you "digest" complex concepts and apply what you've read to your eating problems. These questions aren't a test and there are no right or wrong answers, just as there are no right or wrong feelings. Because a variety of concepts are explored in each chapter, this section is meant to summarize, highlight, and augment learning. It's also intended to probe your inner landscape and (gently) force you to deal with your issues.

If there are questions which are too painful or upsetting, please at least make an attempt to put *something* down on paper, even if it's as simple as "hurt" or "too scary." These are authentic, deeply felt responses and entirely appropriate. If you have difficulty giving a fuller answer, return to the question another time—*and keep returning until you can answer the question thoroughly and completely.* Pushing yourself to be uncomfortable is the name of the game and will help stretch and build emotional muscle. Remember, you're not reading this book to stay the same—your goal is to grow. Like the old AA adage says, "Nothing changes if nothing changes."

One last word of advice. Initially, it may be scary to get in touch with feelings you've kept at bay for decades. If you're in therapy or a support group, please let your group leader know that you're using this workbook. You might also share your discoveries and fears with an understanding friend or two so that they can help you deal with any distress that surfaces. Telling friends also will give you practice reaching out, unburdening, and expressing your feelings to others. Moreover, it will help reduce shame about your eating problems as you work to overcome them.

With practice and patience, both feelings and food will begin to serve you the way they were intended: feelings as a way to nourish your emotional needs and food as a way to nourish your body. As you grow and change, you'll become more whole and more authentically you. In time, you'll wonder how you lived so long without honoring your feelings and you'll begin to effectively take care of all your hungers.

Food & Feelings Pre-Assessment

This assessment tool is designed to help you better understand the nature of your problems with food and feelings. It's a gauge of your strengths and weaknesses in these areas. There are no right or wrong responses. It will give you information about specific behaviors and attitudes you need to change to become a "normal" eater and handle your emotions effectively.

At the end of this book, you'll find a *Food & Feelings Post-Assessment* to be completed when you've finished reading. It contains the same statements as the *Pre-Assessment*. Comparing your responses from both assessments will tell you how much you learned and changed by reading and using this workbook. The *Post-Assessment* will also point to specific, challenging attitudes and behaviors that need more work for you to recover from disordered eating and become emotionally healthy.

Please give each statement some thought before answering, and be honest. Try not to judge your responses; instead, focus on being curious. Pay attention to feelings that arise (after all, this *is* a book about feelings!) by jotting them down, but don't get too caught up in experiencing them until you've completed the assessment. When you're done with the book, return to the *Pre-Assessment* to explore your feelings more fully.

Instructions: Circle the number that best describes your response to each statement. The number 1 represents *least* or *least often* and the number 10 represents *most* or *most often*. Note that in both assessments the words feelings and emotions are used interchangeably.

FEELINGS

	(least)									(most)
1. I am in touch with my feelings.	1	2	3	4	5	6	7	8	9	10
2. I can generally identify and label what I'm feeling.	1	2	3	4	5	6	7	8	9	10
3. I am accepting of all of my feelings.	1	2	3	4	5	6	7	8	9	10
4. I am willing to experience all of my feelings.	1	2	3	4	5	6	7	8	9	10
5. I understand the purpose of feelings.	1	2	3	4	5	6	7	8	9	10

6. I value all of my feelings. 1 2 3 4 5 6 7 8 9 10
7. I give equal weight to all of my feelings. 1 2 3 4 5 6 7 8 9 10
8. I listen to what my feelings have to tell me. 1 2 3 4 5 6 7 8 9 10
9. I don't judge my feelings. 1 2 3 4 5 6 7 8 9 10
10. I reflect on and try to understand my feelings. 1 2 3 4 5 6 7 8 9 10
11. I am curious about my feelings. 1 2 3 4 5 6 7 8 9 10
12. I believe all feelings are bearable. 1 2 3 4 5 6 7 8 9 10
13. I trust my emotions to help guide my life. 1 2 3 4 5 6 7 8 9 10
14. I am effective at taking care of myself when I'm upset. 1 2 3 4 5 6 7 8 9 10
15. I express my feelings appropriately. 1 2 3 4 5 6 7 8 9 10
16. I can tolerate intense feelings well. 1 2 3 4 5 6 7 8 9 10
17. I don't act out my feelings. 1 2 3 4 5 6 7 8 9 10
18. I have healthy, rational beliefs about feelings. 1 2 3 4 5 6 7 8 9 10
19. I don't let other people tell me what to feel. 1 2 3 4 5 6 7 8 9 10
20. I understand the meaning of projection. 1 2 3 4 5 6 7 8 9 10
21. I understand what defense mechanisms are. 1 2 3 4 5 6 7 8 9 10
22. I understand what transference reaction means. 1 2 3 4 5 6 7 8 9 10
23. I understand what secondary emotions are. 1 2 3 4 5 6 7 8 9 10
24. I can distinguish voluntary from involuntary suffering. 1 2 3 4 5 6 7 8 9 10
25. I don't experience much voluntary suffering in my life. 1 2 3 4 5 6 7 8 9 10
26. I know what signal anxiety is. 1 2 3 4 5 6 7 8 9 10
27. I know that people can't make me feel emotions. 1 2 3 4 5 6 7 8 9 10
28. I know when I'm feeling guilty. 1 2 3 4 5 6 7 8 9 10
29. I feel guilty only when it's appropriate. 1 2 3 4 5 6 7 8 9 10
30. I don't let other people guilt-trip me. 1 2 3 4 5 6 7 8 9 10
31. I handle feeling guilty effectively. 1 2 3 4 5 6 7 8 9 10
32. I express my guilt appropriately. 1 2 3 4 5 6 7 8 9 10
33. I understand the purpose of guilt. 1 2 3 4 5 6 7 8 9 10
34. I know when I'm feeling ashamed. 1 2 3 4 5 6 7 8 9 10
35. I can distinguish guilt from shame. 1 2 3 4 5 6 7 8 9 10
36. I can distinguish shame from embarrassment. 1 2 3 4 5 6 7 8 9 10
37. I feel ashamed only when it's appropriate. 1 2 3 4 5 6 7 8 9 10
38. I know people can't make me feel ashamed. 1 2 3 4 5 6 7 8 9 10
39. I handle feeling ashamed effectively. 1 2 3 4 5 6 7 8 9 10
40. I express my shame appropriately. 1 2 3 4 5 6 7 8 9 10
41. I understand the purpose of shame. 1 2 3 4 5 6 7 8 9 10
42. I know when I'm feeling helpless. 1 2 3 4 5 6 7 8 9 10
43. I accept that I can't avoid feeling helpless sometimes. 1 2 3 4 5 6 7 8 9 10
44. I handle feeling helpless effectively. 1 2 3 4 5 6 7 8 9 10
45. I express helplessness appropriately. 1 2 3 4 5 6 7 8 9 10
46. I understand the purpose of helplessness. 1 2 3 4 5 6 7 8 9 10
47. I know when I'm feeling anxious. 1 2 3 4 5 6 7 8 9 10

48. I understand the purpose of anxiety.	1 2 3 4 5 6 7 8 9 10
49. I handle feeling anxious effectively.	1 2 3 4 5 6 7 8 9 10
50. I express my anxiety appropriately.	1 2 3 4 5 6 7 8 9 10
51. I don't have much signal anxiety.	1 2 3 4 5 6 7 8 9 10
52. I know when I'm feeling disappointed.	1 2 3 4 5 6 7 8 9 10
53. I understand the purpose of disappointment.	1 2 3 4 5 6 7 8 9 10
54. I handle disappointment effectively.	1 2 3 4 5 6 7 8 9 10
55. I express disappointment appropriately.	1 2 3 4 5 6 7 8 9 10
56. I learn from disappointment.	1 2 3 4 5 6 7 8 9 10
57. I know when I'm confused.	1 2 3 4 5 6 7 8 9 10
58. I can distinguish confusion from mixed feelings.	1 2 3 4 5 6 7 8 9 10
59. I understand why people become confused.	1 2 3 4 5 6 7 8 9 10
60. I handle being confused effectively.	1 2 3 4 5 6 7 8 9 10
61. I express my confusion appropriately.	1 2 3 4 5 6 7 8 9 10
62. I know when I have conflicted or mixed feelings.	1 2 3 4 5 6 7 8 9 10
63. I understand the necessity of conflicted feelings.	1 2 3 4 5 6 7 8 9 10
64. I tolerate having mixed feelings well.	1 2 3 4 5 6 7 8 9 10
65. I express feeling conflicted appropriately.	1 2 3 4 5 6 7 8 9 10
66. I know when I'm feeling lonely.	1 2 3 4 5 6 7 8 9 10
67. I understand the purpose of loneliness.	1 2 3 4 5 6 7 8 9 10
68. I handle loneliness effectively.	1 2 3 4 5 6 7 8 9 10
69. I express feeling lonely appropriately.	1 2 3 4 5 6 7 8 9 10

FOOD

70. I can distinguish emotional from physical hunger.	1 2 3 4 5 6 7 8 9 10
71. I experience feelings rather than focus on food/weight.	1 2 3 4 5 6 7 8 9 10
72. I allow myself to feel guilty, not focus on food/weight.	1 2 3 4 5 6 7 8 9 10
73. I allow myself to feel shame, not focus on food/weight.	1 2 3 4 5 6 7 8 9 10
74. I allow myself to feel helpless, not focus on food/weight.	1 2 3 4 5 6 7 8 9 10
75. I allow myself to feel anxious, not focus on food/weight.	1 2 3 4 5 6 7 8 9 10
76. I allow myself to feel disappointed, not focus on food/weight.	1 2 3 4 5 6 7 8 9 10
77. I allow myself to feel confused or conflicted, not focus on food/weight.	1 2 3 4 5 6 7 8 9 10
78. I allow myself to feel lonely, not focus on food/weight.	1 2 3 4 5 6 7 8 9 10
79. I express feelings appropriately without using food.	1 2 3 4 5 6 7 8 9 10
80. I accept that "normal" eaters occasionally use food when they're upset.	1 2 3 4 5 6 7 8 9 10
81. I'm compassionate with myself when I use food inappropriately.	1 2 3 4 5 6 7 8 9 10
82. I turn to people, not a food/weight focus when I'm upset.	1 2 3 4 5 6 7 8 9 10
83. I trust myself not to focus on food/weight when I'm upset.	1 2 3 4 5 6 7 8 9 10
84. My life is emotionally full and satisfying.	1 2 3 4 5 6 7 8 9 10
85. I know food won't make me feel better when I'm upset.	1 2 3 4 5 6 7 8 9 10
86. I try hard not to focus on food when I'm upset.	1 2 3 4 5 6 7 8 9 10

87. If I eat when I'm upset, I can usually stop myself.	1 2 3 4 5 6 7 8 9 10
88. I get my emotional needs met without using food.	1 2 3 4 5 6 7 8 9 10
89. I'm gentle with myself if I use food when I'm upset.	1 2 3 4 5 6 7 8 9 10
90. I listen to whether my body wants to eat or not eat when I'm upset, and either is okay.	1 2 3 4 5 6 7 8 9 10
91. I value nourishing myself with food even when I'm upset.	1 2 3 4 5 6 7 8 9 10
92. I want to be emotionally healthy more than I want to distract myself.	1 2 3 4 5 6 7 8 9 10
93. I'm hopeful that I'll overcome my disordered eating.	1 2 3 4 5 6 7 8 9 10
94. I know that I won't end my disordered eating overnight.	1 2 3 4 5 6 7 8 9 10
95. I acknowledge that to end disordered eating I may need help from a therapist.	1 2 3 4 5 6 7 8 9 10
96. I acknowledge that to end disordered eating I may need to join an eating disorder support group.	1 2 3 4 5 6 7 8 9 10
97. I am aware that unless I'm emotionally healthy, I may end disordered eating and adopt other unhealthy behaviors.	1 2 3 4 5 6 7 8 9 10
98. I can visualize myself being emotionally healthy and a "normal" eater.	1 2 3 4 5 6 7 8 9 10
99. I can visualize being comfortable in my body whether or not my weight "changes when I'm eating "normally."	1 2 3 4 5 6 7 8 9 10
100. I am committed to becoming emotionally healthy and recovering from disordered eating.	1 2 3 4 5 6 7 8 9 10

1

The Function of Feelings

(You Mean There's a Point to All This Misery?)

In our fast-paced, too-much-to-do, get-it-done-yesterday world, our attention is more focused on our behavior than on what's going on within us. We're riveted to what's happening out *there*, rather than what's occurring in *here*. Even if we do occasionally take a moment to reflect, our thoughts generally revolve around what we've done in the past and what we'll do in the future—that is, on our actions.

In fact, the bulk of our daily energy is consumed either by behaving or thinking about how to behave. We make endless lists, ruminate about whether we've said or done the right thing, second guess ourselves over trivial decisions made days or decades ago, agonize over what we should do tomorrow, and keep ourselves on edge anticipating what others will do or want so that we'll know precisely how to respond. Our actions are concrete proof that our existence is meaningful and that we're "good" people. Brainwashed, we believe that we are what we do.

On the rare occasions that our minds finally become still and notice what's going on inside, we may not like what we find. If it's unpleasant, we tell ourselves not to dwell on things we can't change or chide ourselves for being self-absorbed. When we hear whispers of uncertainty or distress, we shrink in panic. When we feel confused, vulnerable, or overwhelmed by these inner whispers, we slam the door to our heart and rush off, seeking certainty in order, comfort in action, and numbness in routine. Life is too short to contemplate our navel for long—there are places to go, people to see, and things to do. And anyway, paying attention to what we're feeling inside is just plain icky. Don't go there, we warn ourselves.

Listen to the disparaging language we use to describe what to do with emotions:

get through it	bury the past
rise above	survive the pain
ignore the hurt	resolve our issues
pull it together	buck up
carry on	keep a stiff upper lip

Can you hear the desperation to brush off the messages from our inner world, the eagerness to shove emotions into a corner, as if they're obstacles to living? If only we could get rid of them, we'd be okay, in control, who we want to be, where we should be. We treat our emotions like trash. Just bag 'em up, and put 'em on the curb.

But what if emotions aren't trash? What if they are actually the bright lights that illuminate our journey toward health and happiness? What if, without them, we're destined to exist as shadows of our authentic selves?

What if emotions are the best things that could ever happen to us?

✓ STOP AND FEEL

Before doing this exercise, and every *STOP AND FEEL*, make sure you are sitting in a comfortable position, and that your body is relaxed. Close your eyes, let go of any extraneous thoughts and take a few deep breaths. And remember, don't rush your answer, but let it surface in its own time.

Are there any emotions you're trying to push away right now? Write down the word, phrase, or sentence that best describes what you're feeling. Make sure you're not labeling a thought such as, "*My brain won't stop,*" and that you're focused an affective sensation, such as "*Boy, am I feeling overwhelmed or confused.*"

____

____

____

What is the purpose of feelings?

From what our culture and families teach us about feelings, you'd think that they're irrelevant or incidental to our well-being at best, that they have no valid function, and are merely annoying distractions. However, feelings actually *do* have a function—a crucial one—for everyone on the planet, today and throughout history. Hard-wired into us, they are an essential part of being human. Imagine a world filled with beings lacking emotions! The name for them is robots (even though some of them can mimic human affect.)

This brings up an important point: If we all have the capacity to feel, then feelings are neither accidental nor incidental and must have an evolutionary purpose.

The function of emotions is to tell us about our internal world, just as senses provide guidance in the external world.

Think about how grateful we are for our senses, how much we value the ability to see, hear, taste, touch, and smell. We don't get angry at our senses or try to ignore them. Instead, we accept them because we've figured out their purpose: to help us negotiate the external world. Hurray for our senses! We'd be in a sorry state—maybe even dead—without them.

When it comes to feelings, though, we're ready to close up shop and go fishing. Emotions scare, puzzle, and confuse us. They drive us to eat, shop, drink, starve, gamble, work, exercise, talk nonstop, live dangerously, and take drugs in order not to feel them. Imagine doing that to avoid your senses! Sounds downright silly, doesn't it?

Well, it's just as silly to avoid your emotions, because their purpose is the exactly the same as that of your senses: *to keep you safe and out of harm's way, to steer you toward what's healthy and life-affirming, and deter you from what's dangerous and life-threatening*. Feelings point us towards what's pleasurable and what's painful so we can make appropriate choices.

Of course, both pleasure and pain are relative, arbitrary, and idiosyncratic to each person. That's why some people are actuaries and some are mercenaries, why there are lion-tamers and librarians, why monks choose to live in a cloistered monastery, and archaeologists wing from continent to continent excavating ruins. People also have varying tolerance for pain: Some will complain at a hangnail, while others will ignore a migraine.

However, despite our differing innate and learned responses, we all share major commonalities. I've never met anyone who jumped for joy at the idea of going to the dentist or who didn't go ga-ga over some kind of picturesque panorama. There's good reason for this. We have a better chance at physical survival if we are biologically programmed to be highly sensitive to both pleasure and pain. Well, believe it or not, we're *also* programmed for emotional survival—if we value and pay attention to them, our feelings will help us live and prosper. The bottom line is that both physical *and* emotional health are required to ensure the success of our species.

To sum up, you cannot live a happy, meaningful, satisfying life without experiencing the full range of feelings—good, bad, or indifferent. If you shut them off, you're asking for trouble, because they're the built-in radar system you need to interact effectively with the world. If you want to lead a rich and fulfilling life, accept that your emotions have a vital purpose and read on.

✓ STOP AND FEEL

Once again, take a minute to gently open up to yourself by relaxing and turning your focus inward. Without judgment, ask yourself the following question:

What are you feeling right now?

____

____

____

How do I know when I have a feeling or an emotion?

An emotion is a sensation that initially develops on a physical level. It can start out a bit vague and fuzzy, turn acute and sharp, erupt like a geyser, or surge over you like a tidal wave. Donald A. Norman, in a fascinating book entitled *Emotional Design: Why We Love (or Hate) Everyday Things*, distinguishes between affect and emotion. He says that affect is a vague sensation that may be either conscious or subconscious, but emotion is the *conscious* experience of such affect. "The queasy, uneasy feeling you might experience, without knowing why, is affect," Norman writes. "Anger at Harry, the used-car salesman who overcharged you for an unsatisfactory vehicle, is emotion."

Affect or sensation becomes emotion when we make meaning of it, that is, when we place a sensation in context and tack on a label. Affect takes us from the general to the specific—what we call emotion. In Norman's example, we recognize the cause of our uneasiness (Harry and his greed) and the emotion it produces: anger (at him and perhaps at our ourselves for ignoring our gut reaction that he was a con artist from the start).

> ***You know you have a feeling when you notice a physical sensation that draws attention to itself.***

Both feelings (or affective sensations) and emotions (conscious identification of a feeling) are part of an organic process. You know you have a feeling when you notice a physical sensation that draws attention to itself. As you become aware of the nature of that feeling, you translate it into a particular emotion. One problem with this process, however, is that affects or feelings often run below our radar screen; we kind of notice them and kind of don't. They flit into our awareness and are gone in a flash. And, even when we're aware of a pounding heart, hollowness in our chest, constricted throat, dry mouth, or tense muscles, we often write them off as mere physical disturbances.

Feelings belong to our primitive defense system and are rooted in our collective biology and the history of the species. They are neurological, biochemical reactions that happen on a cellular level in response to stimuli. They don't require thinking. A bear charges at you and you run like hell due to an innate response called fear. However, if you were Barney the Bear's trainer and Barney lumbered over to you every morning as you set out his slab of breakfast meat, you might experience joy at being greeted by your furry friend. Your understanding of the *context* of the advancing bear influences your response, which, in turn, generates a specific reaction.

Here's another example of affect and emotion. Say you used to be crazy about Ben and every time you saw him, your heart did cartwheels, your knees got weak, and your brain turned to maple syrup. Not surprisingly, you might have labeled this constellation of physical sensations as love or infatuation. But ever since you found Ben cheating on you, you see him and your heart starts to pound, there's a knot in your stomach, your face grows beet red, and a surge of tingling energy shoots through your arms and legs. You now call what you feel hate. Same stimulus, different context.

You know you're experiencing emotion when you're not sick and your body, particularly your major organs—heart, lungs, and intestines—have a strong physical reaction to a stimuli.

Here are some sensations that, illness and medical conditions aside, often suggest emotional reaction:

dry throat	inability to focus or concentrate
fatigue	butterflies in your stomach
shortness of breath	pounding heart
queasiness	a lump in your throat
racing pulse	tightness or hollowness in your chest
flushing	constriction around your eyes

For the purpose of this book, I use the terms *feelings, emotions,* and *affects* fairly interchangeably. When I advise you to feel your feelings, I mean everything from the tiniest flicker of bodily sensation to the most specific descriptive label you can muster. It matters little what name you give them. What's important is your ability to remain vitally aware of what's going on inside your body and that you stay with them long enough to give sensations a label.

✓ STOP AND FEEL

Again, settle yourself into a comfortable position, draw a few deep breaths, and put your focus on self-discovery. Are you feeling curious, excited, upset, impatient, wary, or bored (or anything else) about what you're reading? What physical sensations lead you to this conclusion? Make sure to notice all your physical sensations and not just the one that jumps out at you first. Remember, you may be feeling more than one thing.

____

____

____

☼ PRACTICE EXERCISE

Act It Out

PURPOSE: To connect to how you express yourself

RATIONALE: Some people are so awkward and uncomfortable showing emotion that they're afraid to let any feelings out. This exercise will show you what you look like when you're expressing emotion.

WHAT YOU NEED: mirror

DIRECTIONS: Pick one of the emotions you chose earlier in response to the *Stop and Feel* question and act it out for one minute in front of a mirror as if you're being filmed. Without naming the emotion, use facial expressions, body language, and sounds that express it in such a way that no one could mistake it for any other. Try this exercise with one or two more feelings.

REFLECTION (to be done after completion of exercise): How was the experience of acting out your emotions? Was it hard or easy, fun or difficult, awkward or freeing, better or worse than you expected? If you tried out more than one emotion, did you learn anything about your reactions? Give yourself a few minutes to reflect on what you learned about yourself before reading on.

____

____

____

How can I know exactly what emotion I'm feeling?

Identifying emotions takes awareness and practice. Are you someone who knows all about music, fashion, automobiles, art, cooking, Spain, architecture, or dogs? If so, think about how you gained your expertise. You followed a special interest, studied it closely, and became an expert. If, as a child, you played a game with your siblings of who could identify a car's make and model the fastest, you're probably a whiz at telling a Honda from a Hyundai and a Camry from a Camaro. Identifying and translating your inner world is an acquired skill as well.

You'll improve at recognizing emotions by paying close attention to them. The first step is to tune into physical sensations and wonder why you're having them. I don't mean that every sniffle, body ache, or case of indigestion will lead to an emotional epiphany. But when you get a flash of sensation in your body, it's time to consider that it *may* be a precursor to an emotion.

For example, imagine that just this morning you handed your boss a financial report that showed a steep revenue decline for your department, though you'd promised to turn a profit after that holiday bonus. Now, sitting at your desk, you look up and she's standing in your doorway, report in hand. The cold, panicky sensation you're experiencing is likely fear, as you worry whether you'll get chewed out, need to lay off a subordinate, or maybe even get canned.

Here's another example. You're driving to your daughter's college graduation in a terrific mood. However, as you visualize your little darling receiving her sheepskin, you're suddenly tired and experience an overwhelming urge to turn the car around. Aware of a burning sensation around your eyes, you recall your father dying a week before your own college graduation. Still missing his support and love, you're grief-stricken by the memory and realize that your tiredness has nothing to do with your daughter graduating in the present and everything to do with your own graduation long past.

LIST OF EMOTIONS

Use the following list of common emotions when you are vague or uncertain about what you're feeling and want a specific label for it. Note that even though some of these emotions are viewed as positive, they still may make *you* uncomfortable (for example, when you feel flattered or proud of yourself). If you're unskilled at identifying what you're feeling inside, review the list whenever you have a sensation that you want to decipher. Be as specific as you can when naming emotions—*grief* not just sadness, *rage* not mere annoyance, *ecstasy* not plain old happiness, *confusion* not garden-variety unease.

ABANDONED
ADMIRED
AFRAID
AMAZED
AMUSED
ANGRY
ANNOYED
ANXIOUS
APATHETIC
APPRECIATED
APPREHENSIVE
ASHAMED
AWED
AWKWARD
BASHFUL
BETRAYED
BITTER
BORED
CARED FOR
CONCERNED
CONFLICTED
CONFUSED
CONTEMPTUOUS
CONTENT
CRITICAL
DARING
DEFENSIVE
DEGRADED
DEJECTED
DELIGHTED
DEMEANED
DESPERATE
DETACHED
DISAPPOINTED
DISCOURAGED
DISGRACED
DISGUSTED
DOUBTFUL
DRIVEN
ECSTATIC
EDGY
EMBARRASSED
EMPTY
ENTHUSIASTIC
ENVIOUS
EXCITED
EXCLUDED
FEARFUL
FED UP
FORTUNATE
FRAGILE
FRANTIC
FREE
FRUSTRATED
GLOOMY
GRATEFUL
GUILTY
HAPPY
HELPLESS
HOPEFUL
HOPELESS
HORRIFIED
HOSTILE
HUMILIATED
HURT
IGNORED
IMPASSIONED
IMPATIENT
INADEQUATE
INCLUDED
INCOMPETENT
INDIFFERENT
INDIGNANT
INFERIOR
INVALIDATED
INVISIBLE
IRRITATED
JEALOUS
JOYFUL
LETHARGIC
LONELY
LOVED
MAD
MANIPULATED
MISUNDERSTOOD
MIXED UP
NEGLECTED
NERVOUS
OPPRESSED
OVERBURDENED
OVERWHELMED
PANICKY
PASSIONATE
POPULAR
POWERLESS
PROUD
REBELLIOUS
REGRETFUL
REJECTED
RELAXED
RELIEVED
REMORSEFUL
RESENTFUL
RESPECTED
SAD
SERENE
SHOCKED
SHY
STRONG
SUPPORTED
SURE
SUSPICIOUS
TENDER
TENSE
TERRIFIED
THREATENED
TRAPPED
UNAPPRECIATED
UNCERTAIN
UNDERSTOOD
UNDERVALUED
UNHAPPY
UNLOVED
UNPOPULAR
UNSURE
UPSET
USED
VALIDATED
VENGEFUL
VULNERABLE
WEAK
WORRIED
WORTHLESS
WORTHY

Gradually you'll train yourself to translate what you're feeling in your body into what you're experiencing in your heart. Strong physical sensations can mean that information is incoming and that you'd better wake up and smell the coffee. If you check your e-mail, mailbox, Internet headlines, voice mail, and fax machine regularly to see what's coming in and going on, so why ignore the signals from your heart? Eventually, by focusing and labeling specific emotions, you'll establish neural connections that will do the work for you more automatically. As an extra bonus (and one of the key points of this book) by making this connection, you'll also become more conscious of what's going on in your body around food.

✓ STOP AND FEEL

By now, you may not need me to help you transition from reading to tuning into your feelings. If so, that's great; you're catching on.

Do you feel encouraged and/or doubtful that you'll ever learn to connect to your feelings and be able to easily identify them? Why do you think you feel this way?

____

____

____

What feelings are normal and what ones are not?

Feelings may be intense or mild, pleasant or painful, dull or acute, transient or long-lasting. However, they are rarely abnormal. What we generally mean when we ask if something—an emotion, thought, or behavior—is normal is whether it's okay to feel, think, or act a certain way. Behind most questions about normalcy lurk darker, more telling ones: Is there something dreadfully wrong with me? Do other people react as I do or am I the only one? Am I a bad person? What will others think of me if they find out how I really think or feel?

If you're concerned about your feelings being normal or abnormal, you probably lacked a solid emotional education, one in which your parents or other important caretakers felt comfortable with a range and intensity of emotions. Like most folks, they were probably uneasy with *their* darker feelings and believed that there was something wrong with *them*. Not surprisingly, they passed this invalid assumption on to you. Barring brain injury, biochemical abnormities, or what we call sociopathy or psychopathology, we are all born with the capacity to feel all our emotions from A–Z. What you've felt, I've most likely felt, as has a French queen circa 1700 or a camel herder in Egypt in 135 BC.

Feelings are one of the myriad of mystical things that bind us together as human beings. We all know sorrow; we all know joy. Great art, music, dance, theatre, and literature move us all in a nearly universal way. For most people, it comes as a huge relief to realize that whatever they're experiencing is normal. Beyond that is the confidence that if others have survived, we can too.

To complicate matters, we have feelings *about* our feelings, meaning, we tend to pass judgment on the ones that make us uncomfortable. That topic will be addressed more fully in *Chapter Two:*

Fear of Feelings. For now, remember that the desire to have normal feelings is based upon the wish to be acceptable to yourself and to those you love, and that the feelings you might label abnormal are probably perfectly natural. If you really want to know if one of them is off the charts, gather up the courage to ask someone who seems emotionally sound if they can relate. If you're still having trouble, then it's time to speak with a therapist who's used to discussing these issues.

✓ STOP AND FEEL

What are you feeling right now?

____

____

____

Can I control my feelings?

The answer to this question is based, in part, on the intensity of the feelings and your reactions to them. When primitive sensations of arousal or inhibition develop, you simply cannot will them away. Nor would you want to, for they might be communicating something vital. Suffice it to say that by the time they reach consciousness and you label them, they're in play, at least for the moment. If the emotion is, say, mild irritation, you can probably talk yourself out of feeling it or distract yourself. But if the emotion is outrage that wells up from the depth of your being, you're going to have to work a great deal harder to alter your mood. In either case, it would be essential to explore *what* you are feeling and *why* before deciding on a particular course of action.

Alternately, if off in the distance you spot someone who looks like the brute who used to bully you in high school, your body may automatically react as if threatened automatically. Your unconscious, harm-sensing apparatus is doing its job and there's little you can do to control your feelings. As the person draws nearer, however, you may be relieved to discover a complete stranger who has only a slight resemblance to the guy who used to push you around. Alternately, if the person approaching turns out, in fact, to be the school bully, but he looks frail and pathetic, you may experience pity in addition to instant relief.

The most effective way to manage feelings is by altering the beliefs that underlie them. If it's your birthday and everyone in the office has gone home without recognizing the occasion, you may choose to believe that they don't care a fig about you and, consequently, feel disappointed. But if you change your thinking and realize that people might not even know it's your birthday or might have skipped out early due to an impending blizzard, you'll feel less rejected and unhappy.

The process I've just described comes from a therapeutic change model called Cognitive-Behavioral Therapy, which is based on the principle that *your beliefs create your feelings and your feelings produce your behaviors*. If you truly want to benefit from your emotions, you'll have to do a thorough, extensive examination of your belief system to see which thoughts lead to which affects. However, please understand that the goal is not necessarily to control feelings, although that's one way of handling them.

> *The goal is to understand feelings and let them, along with sound judgment, dictate what needs to be done.*

Sometimes you want to experience an emotion to the max, for example, when you're grieving the recent loss of a loved one. Other times you're looking to gain insight into an emotion to understand how you got yourself into an unhealthy situation, such as being dumped by yet another lover. Often you'll want to consider your available options for taking action before, say, tossing out a snide comment that might provoke an argument with your spouse.

The only time that exerting control over emotions is appropriate is when you're in circumstances in which it is unsuitable, and even counterproductive, to express them. If you're in the midst of teaching a geography lesson or about to make a sales pitch and feel overcome with regret for some cutting remark you made to your mother that morning, you'll want to contain your feelings. If you're enraged at a motorist who cuts you off, you'll most certainly want to reign in your anger. If you just escaped a burning building with your three-year-old in your arms, you'll want to take a few deep breaths rather than lose yourself to hysteria.

☼ PRACTICE EXERCISE

Feelings Ladder

PURPOSE: To learn that you have the ability to heighten or decrease the intensity of your feelings by changing your thinking and self-talk.

RATIONALE: When you're upset, you can often calm yourself with comforting words said in a soothing tone. The ability to alter the intensity of feelings makes them easier to bear.

WHAT YOU NEED: imagination

DIRECTIONS: Pick an emotion that you have difficulty experiencing, say, anger or helplessness, and imagine yourself at the bottom of a ladder. Where you're standing is a zone of mild intensity; at the top of the ladder is the peak of the emotion. When you've connected to an emotion, picture yourself slowly climbing the ladder, deliberately intensifying the feeling with each step. You'll know you've reached the top when the feeling swells in your body, as if it's inhabiting every cell. Stay at the top of the ladder for a moment, then slowly talk yourself down, lowering the intensity of feeling until you reach the ground. Practice this exercise with three different emotions.

REFLECTION (to be done after completion of exercise): Take a moment to reflect on how this exercise went. Were you frightened? Did you rush through it? Was it less scary than you expected? Did you have an easier or harder time with one of the emotions you chose? What did you learn about your ability to handle intense feelings?

____

____

____

Why won't bad feelings simply go away?

The truth is, there's actually no such thing as a "bad" feeling. By labeling a feeling negatively, what you mean is that it causes you to feel badly (that is, not pleasurably), or that experiencing it makes you feel as if you're a bad person. Feelings are feelings, just as colors are colors and musical notes are musical notes (and food is food). Think of affects as clouds that have no intrinsic value; whether you welcome them or not is situation-dependent. A cloud blocks out the sun on a scorcher of a day in the middle of a ten-mile hike and you're overjoyed for the respite. A cloud comes along while you're sunbathing and you're momentarily bummed out. How you feel about the clouds is relative, all in your perspective. The same is true of emotions.

If you're wondering why feelings that generate discomfort—what you might call "bad" feelings—won't go and stay away, that's another question entirely and makes me wonder what you believe about emotions. If you believe you're always supposed to feel good, then feeling bad is sure to upset your apple cart. *You're not supposed to feel good all the time; it's simply not possible.* You—we all—have a range of emotions that come and go and that's the way life is supposed to work. If your colleague blames you for something that's not your fault, you'll probably feel misunderstood. If you've been ignoring your brother for months, you may feel ashamed or guilty; if your best friend steals your girlfriend, you'll likely feel betrayed; if you didn't get the job you thought was a shoo-in, there's a good chance you'll feel disappointed. In all of these instances, you'll feel badly. But these feelings *do* eventually go away. Of course, the problem is that they'll come back again in another circumstance because that's the way the emotional ball bounces.

We only brush away our feelings if we don't understand their function and value their purpose—if we forget that they exist, for the most part, to instruct us.

> *To become a whole, healthy person, you have to stop trying to avoid feeling badly and welcome all your emotions without judgment, no matter what they are.*

It might seem hard to imagine right now, but perhaps some day you'll be glad you can embrace feeling helpless, disappointed, sad, lonely, or confused. It will mean that you are functioning appropriately, that you possess the ability to be honest with yourself, that you've reached a high level of consciousness and emotional maturity, and that you no longer have to live in terror of what's inside of you. Imagine what *that* would feel like!

I guarantee that understanding and experiencing your full range of emotions will change your life. You'll no longer have to search in restaurants, supermarkets, the refrigerator, a co-worker's candy dish, or your kitchen cabinets for emotional sustenance and nourishment. Happiness will no longer come in a box, bag, container, carton, jar, or can. It won't arise from a magical number on the scale or the false pride and fleeting high of rejecting food.

By knowing what you feel, you'll know what you need—calm and quiet, risk and excitement, a warm body, a hug, a challenge, to tell off your boss, space of your own, a piano, community, children, work, a good cry, a sense of accomplishment, to return to college, marriage, divorce, a vacation in the mountains, a puppy, to move to Alaska, to grieve your losses, to paint, a trip around the world, to dive head first into your future and shout, "Get ready 'cause here I come!"

Think of accepting your feelings as a "two-fer." You'll be substituting a new feeling focus for your old obsession with food and you'll be getting more out of life, to boot!

✓ STOP AND FEEL

What are you feeling about learning to handle distressing and uncomfortable emotions?

____

____

____

FURTHER EXPLORATION

These questions will help you "digest" the material in this chapter and deepen your understanding about food and feelings. Your responses are an important part of learning more about emotions in general and yours in particular. Please write down your answers.

1. How do you feel about having "bad" feelings? (e.g., afraid, bewildered, confused, annoyed, disconnected, mystified, curious, ashamed, mixed)

____

____

____

2. What do you think is the purpose of feelings?

____

____

____

3. By describing physical sensations, how do *you* know you have a feeling?

____

____

____

4. What are three beliefs you have about feelings being normal/abnormal and/or natural/unnatural?

____

____

____

5. How do you generally react to uncomfortable, upsetting feelings?

____

____

____

6. Why don't "bad" feelings magically disappear?

____

____

____

7. How will you become healthier by changing your beliefs about feelings and your attitude toward them?

____

____

____

8. What would your life be like if you had no feelings?

____

____

____

9. What do you expect your life will be like when you handle feelings effectively?

____

____

____

2

Fear of Feelings

(Can't I Learn to Outrun Them?)

Let's face it. We're all a bit intimidated by emotions. When we're very young, we're entirely at their mercy. Because our brain isn't fully developed in childhood, especially our frontal lobes, the capacity for judgment and the ability to self-soothe are beyond our grasp. These capacities expand as we grow. In fact, experts say that our frontal lobes don't reach full maturation until we're between 20 and 30! Therefore, absent the part of our brain that helps us judge and reason, we have no accessible, internal way to modulate distressing feelings. Without the ability to label emotions, we lack even the small comfort of recognizing that other people feel as we do—terrified, overwhelmed, scared. No wonder feelings are so fearsome.

As babies, we're a stew of sensations, bubbling up and often over, falling into exhausted sleep after minutes or hours of crying our hearts out. The slightest thing can set us off. As children, our emotions are the monsters we can't cram back into the closet, the spidery, tentacled demons that reach out to drag us under the bed, the specters outside the window that threaten safe slumber and sweet dreams. Our young selves lack both the cognitive ability to comprehend that emotions are only one aspect of our totality and sufficient personal history to recognize their transient nature. In fear, we experience our emotions; in fear, we await their return.

Sometimes even as adults we feel emotionally fragile, and our feelings continue to loom large. The truth, however, is that experiencing them won't kill us, drive us crazy, or ruin our well-oiled lives. It will, instead, carry us to a better place. When we have the security to trust emotions as inner guides and the conviction that they're here to help, fear dissolves and curiosity opens our hearts. All we need is the patience to listen and the courage to hear.

✓ STOP AND FEEL

Are you frightened that if you start experiencing intense feelings, you'll be scared, overwhelmed, and unable to handle them?

____

____

____

☼ PRACTICE EXERCISE

Time Travel

PURPOSE: To connect to a painful feeling you had as a child

RATIONALE: Sometimes you may not realize that you can handle the pain of childhood far better now than when it occurred. When you know that you can tolerate emotions that were previously unbearable, experiencing them becomes a whole lot easier and less scary.

WHAT YOU NEED: two photographs of yourself—one as a child and one at your present age

DIRECTIONS: Find a photograph of yourself when you were a child, say, age five or older. If you can locate one in which you're looking (or recall feeling) unhappy, all the better. Give yourself a few minutes staring at the photo to become that unhappy/scared/confused child. Plunge into the feeling. When you've gone as far as you can go, put the child photo face down and bring yourself back to the present by studying the photo of you now. Be conscious of how many decades have passed since your childhood photo was taken and how you can take care of yourself now in ways you could not back then. If you're dissatisfied with your care-taking abilities, remind yourself that you now have other sources (people, books, workshops, therapists) to go to for help and support that you didn't have way back when. What makes you believe you can handle the pain of childhood memories now, or what makes you believe you can't?

____

____

____

REFLECTION (to be done after completion of exercise): What were your reactions to each photo? Did they surprise you? If so, in what way? Do you still feel like that child in the photograph trapped in an adult body? What will it take to convince you that you *can* take care of yourself?

____

____

____

Are all feelings created equal?

According to Sigmund Freud's pleasure principle, we move toward pleasure and away from pain. This theory states that human beings have an innate, internal drive that propels us toward what feels good and an equal, innate drive that repels us from what feels bad. Using CAT scans, today we can even view the parts of the brain that researchers call our pleasure and pain centers, that is, the areas that light up when exposed to pleasurable and painful sensations.

No dummies, we humans naturally prefer enjoyable feelings—joy, delight, contentment, ecstasy, happiness, excitement, love—to distressing ones—hate, despair, remorse, powerlessness, loneliness, anxiety, frustration. So, on the face of things, it would seem that all feelings are *not* created equal. It's evident that some emotions lift us up and others drag us down, and we know which ones are going to win a popularity contest and which will be the wallflowers.

However, *on a deeper level, all feelings really are created equal because each has the same function—to transmit information*. It's not their fault that some come in a more attractive package than others. So be warned, if you're determined to only feel good and never feel bad, you're obstructing feelings from doing their job. If you're screening out the upsetting ones, the truth is that you're not doing *your* job of letting them teach you what you need to know!

My hunch is that there's a high correlation between running from your pain and your disordered eating. What do *you* think? If you're just plain scared of your emotions or feel overwhelmed when they hurt and hurt bad, focusing on food, or on restricting your food, seems like the perfect escape. Unfortunately, out of fear and ignorance, you end up targeting the wrong organ: You should be zeroing in on your heart, not your mouth!

The more you recognize why you avoid your feelings, the better your chance of learning to accept each one with an open heart. The irony is that if you give them half a chance, your deepest heartaches might just pave the way to your greatest happiness.

☼ *PRACTICE EXERCISE*

Color Me Emotional

PURPOSE: To flesh out shades of emotions

RATIONALE: Because certain feelings are scary, we tend to back off from experiencing them. This exercise will help you engage with emotions without inhibition while noticing their subtle gradations.

WHAT YOU NEED: emotions list, colored pencils, paints or chalk, paper

DIRECTIONS: Choose three emotions from the list in Chapter 1 (on page 25) Pick a color for each emotion, whichever seems right for you, and create a picture that expresses that feeling using only that color. When you're done, choose a different color to make another picture of the same emotion that's more intense. Finally, choose yet another color and create a picture with less intensity. See how it feels toning down an emotion (say, from screaming red to soft yellow) or ratcheting it up (say, from a cool blue to a sunburst orange). Now, go through the process with two more emotions.

REFLECTION (to be done after completion of exercise): Did changing colors alter your connection to an emotion? What was it like to try shift intensities? Which emotions gave you the most difficulty?

____

____

____

Do I have feelings about my feelings?

We have emotional reactions to almost everything we think, do, say, imagine, and remember—so the short answer is yes. In fact, many times, it's your feelings *about* your feelings, what we call *secondary emotions* that are the most troubling and cause the most discomfort. *Secondary feelings are reactions, usually unconscious and judgmental, to our primary emotions.* You're angry at yourself for being jealous of your sister, scared that you're too insecure to change jobs, ashamed that you still feel upset about self-destructive behavior you engaged in decades ago. There are any number of permutations of primary and secondary feelings that can worsen your original feeling. It's as if you're standing in an endless hall of mirrors that reflect only the negative—you feel bad about feeling bad about feeling bad and on and on into infinity.

Unfortunately, growing up in this culture, even with parents who have reasonable emotional intelligence, we often find ourselves caught up in judgmental secondary emotions. Society values a stiff upper lip and glorifies the macho ideals of playing down feelings, going it alone, and being in control. Sadly, this only exacerbates emotional pain in the long run and prevents it from being healed. That which is truly healthy and healing—feeling deeply—is valued as unhealthy, while that which is actually unhealthy—pretending not to have pain—is valued as healthy. How crazy is that? No wonder emotions send us scurrying to the refrigerator or to the scale.

If secondary emotions didn't exist, you'd be neutral about whatever you felt. Reactions to feelings would tilt neither one way nor the other. You'd say to yourself: *Okay, so I'm furious/hurt/sad/helpless/anxious/confused. So what? I feel what I feel.* Gone would be the self-punishing insults, the harsh self-critiques, the I-should-feel decrees. You'd no longer measure yourself against some inhuman standard of perfection.

It's hard enough to cope with primary feelings, which, unfortunately, have to be felt (even painfully) to help and heal. It's an impossible task if you insist on constantly criticizing what goes on in your inner world. Although you can't control everything you feel, you can certainly tone down your judgments. Secondary emotions are based on faulty logic and irrational beliefs and often function well below our level of awareness. Living in this culture, we all have them to greater or lesser extent, which means we all need to practice keeping internal negative chatter to a minimum.

✓ STOP AND FEEL

What secondary feelings (such as disgust, disappointment, contempt, or anger) do you have about what you are feeling right now?

____

____

____

Is there one secondary emotion that generally emerges when you feel something deeply?

____

____

____

How did I learn to fear my feelings?

Aside from cultural messages we pick up along the way from teachers, extended family, clergy, neighbors, media, celebrities, books, politicians, and the medical world, most of what we believe about feelings comes from our parents or primary caregivers. Usually, our first lessons came from observing how the people closest to us handled *their* feelings. In many families, feelings are never discussed. I know of instances in which clients have lost a sibling or parent, and life went on as if the death had never occurred. Lips were sealed and neither the death itself nor the deceased were ever mentioned again. What message might this kind of dysfunctional scenario suggest? That feelings are wrong to have and should never be expressed.

Also, many of us associate strong affect with discord and fighting or even physical harm, confusing *feeling* angry with *behaving* angrily. You may have had a parent whose feelings constantly overflowed and who unduly burdened, frightened, and embarrassed others—especially young you—whenever they unloaded. Maybe you wanted to clap your hands over your ears and hide in a corner whenever they let loose. Somewhere along the way you then made an unconscious decision to never lose control of your emotions and embarrass yourself or scare others in this way. Or if you were raised in a family in which your parents constantly argued, any level of conflict might frighten you now. Although you're safe as an adult (because you're no longer dependent upon your battling parents), the fragile child inside still withdraws into a shell or becomes paralyzed around interpersonal tension and conflict.

Or your household may have appeared healthy and normal, but you were frequently scolded for expressing unhappiness or encouraged to always look on the bright side. You were told to stop crying or fussing, be a big girl or boy, not make such huge a deal of things, quit being such a baby.

If your parents insisted that you always be Marty or Mary Sunshine, the message you received was that "negative" emotions were wrong and that you'd better keep a lid on them if you want to get along (read, *be loved* by others). So you became an expert in what psychology calls "acting as if" by encasing your authentic self in a public shell designed to please the crowd.

In families where your caregivers could say whatever they damned well pleased, but jumped down your throat every time you piped up, you were given a double message: It's okay for *other* people to express their feelings, but you'd better zip *your* lip—or else. If your parents gave you the silent treatment whenever you displayed irritation or sadness, you might believe that your anger or grief will always lead to rejection, abandonment, and withdrawal of love.

Invalidating comments such as, "Of course you don't feel like that" or, "You shouldn't feel that way," might cause you to doubt and mistrust your inner voice. If you were told repeatedly by someone in authority that you did not feel what you knew you felt, you probably ended up a very confused little boy or girl. And, unless the message was revised somewhere along the way, you may have grown up into (and still be) a very confused man or woman. And speaking of confusion, if you watched a parent that you viscerally knew was unhappy pretend to be happy, you might not have known *what* to think: Do you believe what your parent says or your gut and intuition?

Although we receive training in everything from driving a car to taking the SATs, nowhere are we formally schooled in how to handle feelings. When we're young, we watch what big people do, and respond according to their expectations. We haven't the foggiest idea whether they're instructing us well or poorly. In fact, we have no idea they're teaching us at all (and, unfortunately, neither do they). However, like good little soldiers, we become well trained, often by the time we're ready to go to school, and unless we learn something to the contrary about how to handle emotions, we grow up with attitudes that are strikingly similar to our parents.

The fact that these attitudes may not be workable or may be downright destructive usually fails to occur to us until we find ourselves drinking, drugging, overeating, intentionally starving, ruining relationships, lacking friends or intimacy, or anxious and depressed. At some point, we realize that all is not well in the land of emotions. If we're lucky enough to believe it's okay to get help, we find someone—a friend or professional—to talk with about our situation. But if we were taught that feelings should be kept private because they're shameful and make us vulnerable, we suffer in silence.

Now let me give you a terrific example of what I consider excellent emotional schooling, an interaction I overheard in a department store many decades ago. This anecdote will give you something with which to compare your emotional education. Late one afternoon, a mother and toddler were in the dressing room next to mine and I could hear the poor little tyke complaining that he wanted to go home. He got crankier by the minute until he started to bawl. His mother tried to comfort him, but he wasn't buying it. Finally, he screamed at the top of his lungs, "I hate you, I hate you. I want to go home." To be honest, I tensed, ready to hear her scold him, but instead the mother said gently, "I know, sweetie, you're angry at Mommy. Mommy's taking an awfully long time and you want to go home. I don't blame you at all for being angry and hating Mommy right now."

Amazing, right? Now, let's look at what this little guy might have learned: that it's okay to be angry, that someone cared about his feelings, that other people can take responsibility for causing hurt, and that feelings are natural and acceptable. When his mother validated his anger, he also got the message that another person interpreted his feelings exactly as he did. And by her repeating that he hated her "right now," he was learning that she believed his feeling would go away and wasn't a permanent state of being.

Compare this interaction with what *could* have happened when the toddler screamed that he hated his mother. What would he have internalized if she'd started yelling at him to shut up, stop being so impatient, or quit being a crybaby? Worse, what if she'd smacked him? He would have internalized that his feelings didn't matter, that it's okay for her to be angry but not okay for him, that his anger upsets other people and gets him into trouble, that what he was feeling was very wrong, and, worst of all, that he was bad and unlovable for expressing himself.

Which kind of parents did you have? Were they like the one in the dressing room or the ones I just described? Whichever model you had will have a direct and decisive bearing on how you feel about your emotions today.

Sometimes we have no idea that what we learned in childhood is unhealthy until our feelings are treated respectfully. Decades ago I took a workshop in which participants partnered up to re-enact a troubling, emotionally-upsetting incident from childhood that involved our parents. The goal was to recreate the interaction, not the way it actually happened, but the way we *wished* it had happened so that our needs had been met. Each partner took a turn being parent and child, and by the end of the exercise, we were all wet-eyed. It was eye-opening and heart-breaking to have a stranger tend to our wounds and to realize how each situation could have been handled so much more effectively by our childhood caregivers.

Sadly, as a therapist, I'm often the first person who listens to someone's feelings—not only listens, but validates, understands, explores, explains, supports, and soothes.

✓ STOP AND FEEL

Are you having any emotional reaction to memories of how your parents or caregivers mishandled their emotions or yours?

____

____

____

PRACTICE EXERCISE

Revamping the Past

PURPOSE: To connect with a painful incident from childhood

RATIONALE: Playing out painful childhood memories the way they happened and then the way you wish they had happened is a way of getting in touch with and freeing up distressing emotions.

WHAT YOU NEED: childhood memories, your voice

DIRECTIONS: Select a childhood incident that your parents handled poorly and which you vividly remember. Speaking aloud, tell yourself the story the way it actually happened, making the memory as strong as possible. Without judgment, pay attention to feelings that arise. Stay focused on how badly you felt back then and perhaps still feel. Now retell the story the way you wish your parents had handled the incident. Again, without judgment, pay attention to the feelings that surface. Try this technique with any troubling scenes from childhood.

REFLECTION (to be done after completion of exercise): Were you able to connect with your feelings from this incident? Was it too painful, even today, to experience them for long? Did you have trouble not judging your parents or yourself? What emotions surfaced when you retold the story with your needs being met?

____

____

____

How can I learn to accept all of my feelings?

In each chapter on specific feelings and in *Chapter 12: Freeing Your Feelings*, you'll learn exactly what to do with emotions, including how to become more accepting of them. For now, here's a general outline to get you started.

First, acknowledge that, as a person who intentionally and regularly rejects or consumes food to distract from feeling, you most likely have a negative view of uncomfortable emotions. This won't be a surprise to many of you. But for some, this may be shocking news, as you may not have seen your food or weight focus as a way to avoid distress.

Second, identify exactly what you believe about emotions. A belief, sometimes called a cognition, is what you hold true about yourself and the world. Let's call it *your* truth, but not necessarily *the* truth. We internalize beliefs in childhood and tend to cling to them tenaciously even when they're not working for us. As you consider your beliefs, try to remember the exact phrases your parents used when responding to your distress. It's those words that are lodged in your head today wreaking all sorts of havoc. Notice in particular the beliefs that are unhealthy and irrational, that is, the ones that don't contribute to emotional balance and resilience, to being an authentic person, to trusting yourself, to enjoying intimacy in relationships, and to having positive associations to food, eating and your body.

Third, make a conscious, ongoing effort to change your beliefs. That means developing your own cognitions about emotions. It doesn't matter what anyone else believed way back when or what your partner or friends believe now. You no longer *have* to drink your milk or go to bed before your favorite TV show is over and you certainly don't have to take someone else's word for the right way to view feelings. Even mine! You're one of the big people now, and you can choose to believe whatever you please.

When I ask you to accept your uncomfortable emotions, I'm not suggesting that you walk around in a perpetual state of hatred, gloom, or shame. Acceptance does not mean letting them run you ragged or having a field day with other people. Nor does it imply that you must *like* having unsettling and sometimes acutely wounding emotions. It merely requires that you acknowledge the hurt and give unpleasant feelings the right to come and go, just as you do the pleasant ones. Think of it as all's fair in love—and pain!

Effective emotional management starts with a sound, rational belief system. That means digging deep, not only into your assumptions about feelings but into understanding how these beliefs have shaped your emotional life and dysfunctional eating behaviors. For example, if you believe that emotions make you vulnerable and weak, you won't be able to stop pushing them away (or stop using an obsession with food and weight to avoid them) no matter how hard you try.

Emotions are natural and provide you with valuable information about yourself.

However, if you believe that emotions are natural, that they provide you with valuable information about yourself and your life, and that you can handle whichever ones come along, you'll be paving the way to healing your disordered eating once and for all. Remember, you can't change the behavior unless you change the belief underlying it. All it takes to transform your perspective is motivation, awareness, time, patience, and practice. I can't stress strongly enough that *accepting your emotions, however painful they are, is the key not only to ending dysfunctional eating but also to achieving the health, happiness, success, and deep satisfaction about life you want and deserve.*

RATIONAL AND IRRATIONAL BELIEFS

Here's a list of unsound, irrational beliefs (IB) about emotions that have been reframed (think "same picture, different frame") to make them sound and rational (RB).

IB: Some emotions are wrong to feel.
RB: Emotions are neither right nor wrong.

IB: If I feel my feelings, I'll be overwhelmed by them.
RB: I can learn to handle any feelings I have.

IB: I shouldn't have bad feelings about another person.
RB: If someone hurts me, it's okay to have negative feelings about them.

IB: Feelings are private and shouldn't be discussed.
RB: It's important to share feelings with people who will value and understand them.

IB: If I show my true feelings, people will humiliate, shame, or punish me.
RB: Only unhealthy people would humiliate, shame, or punish me for showing my true feelings.

IB: If I hurt other people's feelings, they'll retaliate and try to hurt me back.
RB: Only unhealthy people would retaliate when their feelings are hurt.

IB: Feelings won't change anything, so why bother to feel or express them?
RB: Feelings may not change situations, but experiencing and expressing them is my right and can change me for the better.

IB: No one cares how I feel.
RB: There are many healthy people in the world who care how I feel.

IB: If I start to feel my feelings, I'll lose it.
RB: I can learn to handle even the most intense emotions.

IB: People who whine about feelings are weak, silly, needy complainers.
RB: Expressing and sharing feelings is normal and an act of courage.

IB: If I ignore my feelings, they'll go away.
RB: My feelings exist to provide me with wisdom about my life.

IB: If I were strong, I wouldn't have problems with my feelings.
RB: True inner strength comes only from coming to terms with feelings.

IB: My feelings are too painful to bear.
RB: I can bear any feeling with practice and help from others.

This list is by no means exhaustive, but should give you an idea of what irrational beliefs sound like and how to change them into rational ones.

☼ PRACTICE EXERCISE

Bye Bye Irrational Beliefs

PURPOSE: To get rid of irrational beliefs about feelings

RATIONALE: The first step to bearing and effectively handling difficult emotions is to purge your irrational beliefs about them.

WHAT YOU NEED: At least a dozen small pieces of paper (about 2" by 2"), pen or pencil, garbage can

DIRECTIONS: Write an irrational belief on each piece of paper. Don't stop until you have at least a dozen. When you're done, read each one aloud, then rip it into tiny pieces and throw it away (or put it through a shredder) while saying emphatically, "That's not true." Smile broadly as each belief symbolically disappears from your life.

REFLECTION (to be done after completion of exercise): What did it feel like to set down your irrational beliefs? What emotions surfaced as you tore or shredded each one? Were you able to connect to joy and relief in letting go of irrational beliefs?

____

____

____

Now that you've gotten rid of your irrational beliefs about emotions (at least symbolically), the next step is to develop a rational belief system that will encourage you to honor, experience, and express your feelings.

☼ PRACTICE EXERCISE

Hello Rational Beliefs

PURPOSE: To create a rational belief system about emotions

RATIONALE: Functional beliefs about emotions lead to experiencing and expressing them in a healthy way.

WHAT YOU NEED: Pen

DIRECTIONS: Review the rational beliefs about feelings listed on the previous pages and write down the ones that you want to believe (maybe all of them!). Use them as is or put them in your own words. Next add your own rational beliefs about emotions. Your beliefs should be in the present, concrete, behavioral, and in the first person. Come up with as many as you can.

RATIONAL BELIEFS ABOUT EMOTIONS:

____

____

____

____

____

____

REFLECTION (to be done after completion of exercise): Was it difficult or easy to reframe your irrational beliefs? How did you do coming up with rational ones? What did you notice about the process of creating healthy beliefs? Reframing beliefs is an ongoing process, so review your beliefs about your emotions frequently.

Ending judgments and negative reactions to your feelings is absolutely essential to curbing disordered eating. Scary as it may be to delve into your emotions, isn't it worse to contemplate spending the rest of your life obsessed with eating or not eating? *To become a healthy person you have to give yourself complete permission to feel the entire spectrum of emotions*. You have a choice. Which will it be?

✓ STOP AND FEEL

How are you feeling about changing your entire emotional belief system?

FURTHER EXPLORATION

1. List the *secondary feelings* you generally have about your feelings or about having feelings.

2. Which feelings do you judge the most harshly?

3. What are three things you usually say to yourself when you're criticizing your feelings?

____

____

____

4. What are three examples that illustrate how your parents or other family members mishandled *their* emotions?

____

____

____

5. What are three examples that illustrate how your parents or other family members mishandled *your* emotions?

____

____

____

6. What are three steps you could take to begin accepting your feelings?

____

____

____

7. What do you expect will be the most difficult aspect of learning to handle your feelings effectively and appropriately (such as getting rid of judgments, changing beliefs, recognizing the destructive effect that your upbringing had on your emotions, tolerating intense affect—or all of the above)?

____

____

____

____

____

____

8. How do you feel regarding what you learned about emotions in this chapter (such as encouraged, disappointed, uneasy, mixed, uncertain)?

____

____

____

3

Feelings, Not Food

(I'd Rather Suck on a Lemon!)

Because feelings are so complicated and we're so poorly schooled in handling them, it's easy to see why anyone might get food and feelings confused. However, if you consistently binge or reject food when you're upset rather than let your feelings flow, you are not meeting your body's needs for nourishment and pleasure or your heart's need to experience its wisdom. Very possibly you don't even realize that your eating behaviors are being driven by internal discomfort. In fact, you may be *so* out of touch with your emotions that you have no idea they even exist, simmering below the surface of consciousness. They're only a heartbeat away, but if you constantly tune them out, they might as well be on the moon!

Remember, feelings are the portal to your inner world, the key to your deepest yearnings and desires, the compass that guides you through life. Focus in on feelings as sharply you do on food and weight obsessions (maybe even *half* as sharply) and you'll get vital information that will move you toward health and authentic happiness. This may seem like a tall order to someone who's depended on dysfunctional eating to quell emotional pain. Yet, there's no other way. Food is food and feelings are feelings, and never the twain shall meet.

If you're tired of searching in supermarkets and restaurants for the cure to what ails you, if you're sick of obsessing about fats and calories or the magic number on the bathroom scale, it's time to find a better way to manage your emotions.

What is the connection between feeding and feeling?

One of the major reasons we focus on food when we're in distress is the powerful primitive connection that exists between feeding and feeling. It's no accident that food becomes an issue when emotional dander starts to fly. If you take a closer look at your earliest years on earth, you'll see that you come by an appetite-affect response quite naturally.

Here's what happens. Nothing is more critical for an infant than being fed. At best, a poorly nourished child will suffer malnutrition; at worst, it will starve to death. An effective parent takes the utmost care feeding an infant: The bottle must be heated to just the right temperature, the baby must be held at the correct angle, and feeding must stop if the baby falls asleep or has had enough.

> ***Nothing is more critical for an infant than being fed.***

Moreover, the physical and emotional bonding that occurs between parent and child during feeding is nearly as crucial as the receipt of adequate nourishment. An innate physical need gets expressed through closeness. Think how most of us like to hold hands, hug, cuddle, fondle, and have sex. Touch often reaches our hidden wounds and comforts us in a way that words simply cannot. Additionally, on a metaphysical level, touch makes us feel less alone in this vast and mysterious universe, offering reassurance that someone is close by.

As infants, we suffer from two mystifying and terrifying human conditions: We're often hungry and we hate being left alone for long. Being fed while we're held is something close to divine. For babies, it just doesn't get any better. (Sometimes for grownups too!) And that's where feeling and feeding first intersect or fuse. When we're lovingly held while receiving nourishment, two of our most urgent needs are gratified at once; hence, most of us begin to associate feeding with safety, security, closeness, pleasure, and comfort. From then on, the two are forever inextricably entwined—married for better or worse.

Moreover, milk, our first meal, is a tasty source of pleasure in its own right. Containing tryptophan, milk produces a relaxing response. Even if we weren't cradled in loving arms as we drank, we couldn't help but make a deliriously delightful, unconscious connection to being fed and a contented drowsiness. And, forever after, this is one of the unconscious attractions that food has for us—the blissful tranquility we felt as infants, something we still, at times, achingly long for.

Some babies, however, are not so fortunate. Their parents are out of sync with their feeding needs or fail utterly to meet them. Infants who remain hungry for too long may associate hunger with extreme emotional discomfort and distress. Or they may be handled roughly when fed, a bottle shoved into their tiny mouth, and forced to drink until it's all gone whether they're full or not. Some babies receive little, if any, positive body contact when fed. In such cases, feeding and feeling are still coupled together, but in a cruel way: Nourishment is associated with punishment and/or literal intrusion, and food may eventually be perceived as discomforting.

It's essential to understand this initial, potent connection between feeling and feeding, especially if you're the kind of disordered eater that comes down really hard on yourself. You think there's something critically wrong with you, that you're defective, weird, weak, unbalanced, or depraved because of the intense, overwhelming urgency or repulsion you feel toward food. Understanding this primitive association makes it easier to suspend judgment after your next binge, or when all you've eaten all day is a lettuce leaf. The key is to recognize that you're biologically programmed to focus on food when under stress. This association is hard-wired, so, please, have some compassion for yourself.

The link goes far beyond infancy, however. Even if it wasn't the case in your particular family, in our culture (and most), food is special and often confers specialness. Parents may serve frozen dinners every night, but when company rings the bell, they generally make an extra effort to serve a tasty and tasteful meal. Food is associated with times of high emotion—candy for Valentine's Day, homemade cookies for a sick friend, a decorative wedding or birthday cake, candy canes hung on a Christmas tree, chocolate coins for Chanukah, an array of dishes on the dining room table after a funeral, and a traditional turkey that brings family home for Thanksgiving. Everywhere we turn, food is smack in the middle of occasions that tug at our heartstrings.

In the best of worlds, our parents weren't disordered eaters or obsessed about weight and didn't use a spoon or a scale to keep their inner world from exploding. Instead, they validated our feelings, spent just the right amount of time soothing us, and handled their own feelings competently. They offered us goodies from time to time when we were unhappy, but gave us the message loud and clear that food is the appropriate response to physical hunger, and that friends and family are there for sympathy and support.

The sad truth is I've only met a handful of people who've had parents this insightful, thoughtful, sensitive, and emotionally intelligent.

If you weren't raised in the best of worlds, but like many of us, grew up in your own little world, your appetite-and-emotions connection may be faulty. You may use food to feel better, to avoid feeling worse, or to feel nothing at all. If you fixate on weight and food to avoid emotional wounds, rather than turn to people for support, you have the whole process backwards.

If you want to end disordered eating, you have to break the link between feelings and food.

This is a formidable, arduous task because this connection *is* hard-wired and because of the considerable reinforcement we receive about using food as an emotional Band-Aid.

However, take heart: *This link can be broken.* Through hard work, you can reprogram yourself to form a positive, healthy relationship with your heart and your hunger. I know you can succeed because I've done it myself and helped scores of others do it. But first you have to learn everything you can about your emotions. I mean everything!

✓ STOP AND FEEL

How do you feel about your food problem now that you understand the powerful biological connection between food and feeling?

____

____

____

☼ PRACTICE EXERCISE

Self-Comfort

PURPOSE: To learn to physically self-soothe

RATIONALE: Self-soothing is a necessary skill in regulating emotions, a combination of positive self-talk and receiving physical comfort (even from yourself!).

WHAT YOU NEED: something comfy to sit on

DIRECTIONS: Sit in a comfortable chair or on a stack of big, soft pillows and burrow in until your body feels just right in your cozy nest. Now wrap your arms around yourself and give yourself a gentle hug. Notice how it feels. If it's okay, rub your arms gently, give yourself a pat on the back, or stroke your hair. Say comforting things to yourself. Try to connect your gestures and words with being soothed, and relax into them. It's fine if the exercise feels silly, strange, or makes you uncomfortable. Keep at it until the discomfort dissolves and you relax.

REFLECTION (to be done after completion of exercise): What was it like trying to physically soothe yourself? Did you connect with any comforting experiences from childhood or did your attempts feel foreign or have negative associations? If your reaction was negative, try to understand why you might feel this way.

____

____

____

Why does food taste so good when I feel so bad?

Lets face it—focusing on food is a grand distraction from our troubles. The very activities of searching through cupboards, shopping and cooking, chewing and swallowing, and cleaning up afterwards divert your attention *away* from what's going on inside you *toward* what you're doing. The mental effort of calculating calories and fat grams wipes everything else off your slate. Not that you're necessarily aware of this diversion when you grab a snack when you're not hungry or daydream about the fantastic life you'll have when you lose ten pounds—frankly, you're probably on autopilot. You may be thinking about food not *because* you're upset, but to *prevent* yourself from becoming upset. Vaguely aware of internal alarm, you hurry to shut off distressing sensations before they erupt into consciousness.

If you're a dysfunctional eater who turns toward food when you're feeling bad, it tastes good in part because you're desperately looking for ways to ward off the blues, the blahs, or the jitters. How often do you continue to eat something that's flavorless, barely edible, or downright repulsive—dry cereal, frozen donuts, stale crackers, a tub of butter, rancid leftovers—rather than experience your feelings? Let's face it, you wouldn't order any of these foods in a restaurant, but you tolerate them because a bad taste—any taste—beats a bad feeling any day of the week. Sometimes, what you're swallowing is so horrid that it really is a toss up; but too often, even when you're in doubt, food wins out.

Food is supposed to be appetizing & appealing, delectable & divine.

Another reason that food tastes good for people who view it as a panacea is that it's meant to be eaten so that our species will survive and flourish. Food is supposed to be appetizing and appealing, delectable and divine. So when you bite into a juicy apple or a buttery croissant, it's no surprise that your taste buds cheer wildly. They're happy even if you're not. But just because something tastes good doesn't mean you should be eating it, especially if the real business at hand is attending to emotions.

Science has come a long way in understanding the complexities of appetite and affect. Research tells us that under stress our bodies crave carbohydrates, which have chemical properties to soothe and relax us, just as milk did in infancy. Not only does food taste heavenly, it's also a source of what we're physiologically lacking in moments of distress. Take carbohydrates whose chemical compounds break down in our bodies in such a way as to calm and comfort us. Food does this job extremely well—too well!

If you eat when you're in emotional distress, are you starting to see what you're up against? Is it beginning to make sense why you're drawn toward yummy when you're feeling crummy?

In spite of the fact that food is meant to nourish and be savored, if you're a restrictive or rigid non-eater, you may use food to decrease or avoid emotional turmoil because the act of saying "No" is such a huge chunk of effort and such a validation of being in charge of your life. If you're feeling proud and elated about disciplining yourself to refuse food, there's very little room for upsetting emotion to squeeze into consciousness. Moreover, by rejecting food you're putting your world back in balance as you offset internal agita with self-restraint. The very act of overpowering your innate hunger and craving for nourishment is a way of proving to yourself that you're strong and invulnerable.

As you've learned, this is an exceedingly complicated subject that involves both body chemistry and early nurturing.

✓ STOP AND FEEL

How does understanding the link between food and feeling lessen your shame about your disordered eating?

____

____

____

Is it ever okay to overeat or skip meals in response to disturbing feelings?

There's nothing unusual or wrong with occasionally turning to or away from food or skipping meals when you're down in the dumps or overwound. It's all in your perspective—the way you think about food and its place in your life. "Normal" eaters may seek a lift in a candy bar or a cannoli, but they know that eating is no magical remedy for the downside of life. They recognize that food can be a savory treat, but will not solve ongoing problems. In fact, "normal" eaters may be terrible problem-solvers, but the one thing they don't regularly do to feel better is stuff themselves or habitually deny themselves nourishment and the pleasure of food.

Moreover, even if they eat when they're frazzled, people who have a healthy relationship with food generally remain at least minimally connected to their bodies, and therefore stop eating when they're full or satisfied. They're just as likely to consume half of what they've chosen as they are to clean their plate. Whatever happens to the food once they're satisfied is of no concern to them.

Of course, even people who are comfortable around food sometimes become so upset that they *do* disconnect from their bodies. What distinguishes them from people with eating problems is that this behavior isn't part of an everyday pattern. They don't beat themselves up, eat in secret, feel shame, or swear to eat differently tomorrow. Their self-concept, self-esteem, and general attitude have nothing to do with their behavior around food.

Most importantly, they wouldn't spend the next hour and a half (or day and a half) chastising themselves or use splurging on a treat as permission to go on a wild food binge. And they certainly wouldn't deprive themselves the next time they were hungry. If you asked what they did when they were distressed, they might not even remember that they'd enjoyed a bag of munchies or skipped an entire meal. They might have secondary emotions about what they were initially *feeling*, but not about what they'd eaten or not eaten. Plus, they'd trust that their appetite would return to normal when emotional equilibrium returned.

On the other hand, even "normal" eaters can truly lose their desire for food when hit with intense emotions. After a shock to the system, their appetite shuts down and the sight, thought, or smell of food may lose its appeal. "Normal" eaters do not intentionally deprive themselves of sustenance and nutrients as a way to cope; the response is automatic and unconscious and, except over an extended period of time, is not self-injurious. If this reaction occurs only occasionally, it's nothing to worry about.

However, avoiding food on an ongoing basis is another story. If your conscious intent is to not eat because you think you'll get fat or won't get thin, or because eating makes you physically and emotionally uncomfortable, you're imposing an unhealthy restriction on your body. Moreover, you may have discovered that one of the best detours around your messy inner world is to shift from your heart to your head by refusing food. Instead of dealing with your life, you reminisce about a thinner past or fantasize about a skinnier future.

Although it's absolutely fine to occasionally use or refuse food when you're feeling low, breaking out into a binge or going on a hunger strike on a regular basis is simply unhealthy. Your work is to trust that you'll gradually move towards eating more normally, and only rarely eat or refuse food when you're upset (with absolutely no remorse!). Which brings me to the subject of realistic expectations. The truth is you're going to need a lot of practice to sever the connection between feeling and feeding. The good news is that you can practice all day long, every day—every time you're hungry or have a craving, every time you sense inner turmoil, every time you start obsessing about food or weight. Each moment is a golden opportunity to work toward getting food and feeling right!

✓ STOP AND FEEL

Are you worried that you'll never be able to choose feeling over dysfunctional eating?

____

____

____

☼ PRACTICE EXERCISE

It's Only Food

PURPOSE: To recognize: 1) what it is about food that attracts/repels when you're in emotional discomfort and 2) how you confer upon food magical powers it doesn't have. (Do this exercise only when you are feeling calm and relatively comfortable with yourself.)

RATIONALE: Most of us have strong feelings about food one way or the other. Recognizing your visceral reactions is a great way to improve your relationship with eating *and* feeling.

WHAT YOU NEED: Food that you are drawn to or repelled by when you have emotional flare ups

DIRECTIONS: Place in front of you a food that you usually eat or overeat, or alternately, one that you intentionally avoid when you're upset. Notice how unmagical the food is, how it's merely a mix of ingredients. Pick it up, smell it, and even play with it. Focus on its composition (e.g., eggs, sugar, wheat, flour) and write what you notice about it. Take a bite and note how the food tastes and feels in your mouth. Concentrate on defusing this food's power and write your reactions to your first bite. Taking a slow second and third bite, continue to write your reactions.

REFLECTION (to be done after completion of exercise): What did you find magical about this food? What did you find ordinary? Exactly what does this food do for you when you are in emotional distress? What tells you that it really has no magic at all?

How can I separate feeling from feeding?

Part of the answer to this question takes us back to *Chapter 1: The Function of Feelings* and how you know you feel emotional pain. If you're fairly accepting of and comfortable with feelings, you'll have an easier time than if you're almost entirely disconnected from them. The more disengaged you are, the earlier in the emotional process you'll have to sit up and take notice. People have varying accessibility to feelings. I've had clients whose typical response to being asked what they were feeling was an "I-don't-know" shrug, and others who could describe in minute detail exactly what was going on inside of them.

How well you separate feeling from feeding depends on where you are on the connected-to-feelings continuum. Stop and think how you'd describe yourself (and how those who know you well would describe you). Are you strongly in touch with feelings, moderately in touch, or out of touch? If you and your emotions rarely take a spin around the dance floor, you'll have to educate yourself about how your bodily sensations translate into emotions. What sensations indicate you're angry? Lonely? Sad? Disappointed? Frustrated? Helpless? Confused? Does each emotion feel the same in your body or does each arise from different physical sensations?

The first step in disengaging appetite from affect is to translate body sensations to emotions. Start by paying specific attention to your breathing, pulse, and energy level. Notice if your chest feels hollow or fluttery, your gut is a tight knot, a hundred butterflies are flitting around your belly, your shoulders are tense, your fists or jaw are clenched, you're spacey or queasy, thoughts are racing around your head, or if there's a sense of dread in the pit of your stomach.

Too often we ignore physical manifestations of emotions rather than recognize them for what they are—messengers sending out a bulletin about what's going on inside of us. Here are some examples. If every time you visit your friends Leann and Scott, they do nothing but bicker, you may feel an unpleasant clenching in your stomach as you're about to ring their bell. If at the last minute you bow out of driving your best friend to the airport because you decide to sleep in, you may suffer a gnawing, nagging feeling that you did something wrong. If you're about to read a letter from the college you're dying to get into and your sister asks you a dumb question, you may feel disconnected from reality and not even hear her. These are all examples of physical reactions that accompany internal distress.

Your response to danger is biologically programmed, and of necessity, highly attention-grabbing in order to keep you alive. When you perceive a threat, your senses automatically perk up, your breathing quickens, and blood flows to your heart, making it pound. The emotions you have when you're robbed at knifepoint are probably a good deal easier to identify than what you're feeling on Saturday night with nothing to do—antsy, mildly anxious, tired, empty, lonely, alienated, sad, or bored.

Some emotions broadcast themselves loud and clear, while others barely whisper, so you'll have to become very still and listen closely to what's going on inside of your body to discover what emotion may be struggling to surface. You can't skip this process.

> *If you want to disengage feeding from feeling, you have to experience the physical sensations that arise within you, no matter how uncomfortable.*

☼ PRACTICE EXERCISE

Physical Manifestations of Emotion

PURPOSE: To connect physical sensations to emotions

RATIONALE: The best way to recognize if an emotion is stirring is to scan your body for physical sensations that you are feeling something deeply.

WHAT YOU NEED: painful memories

DIRECTIONS: Choose a disturbing incident that happened during the past week or one that's been haunting you for ages. Bring your feelings about it into sharp focus. As if you're watching TV, turn up the volume and make sure the picture is clear and bright. Label what you're feeling: dread, shock, rage, remorse, disappointment, powerlessness. Notice the sensations in your body that connect to this emotion. Also note what happens when you label what's going on, especially if the feeling worsens or eases up. Pay attention to what organs or body parts are in play and what's happening to them. Choose another feeling and go through the same process.

REFLECTION (to be done after completion of exercise): Were you able to identify the parts of your body holding your emotion? Do you usually pay attention to this kind of reaction or ignore it? What happened when you gave physical sensation the label of an emotion?

____

____

____

If you're feeling the least bit unskilled at connecting to body sensations that signal emotions, take heart. You have many chapters ahead of you to learn more about how internal commotion is channeled into an emotion. For now, simply pay attention to physical shifts which may indicate internal distress. The next step will be to fine tune and become expert at labeling emotions. This means distinguishing guilt from shame, anger from fear, helplessness from anxiety, confusion from uncertainty.

The final step, what to *do* with emotions, will be laid out in detail in the closing chapters of this workbook. For now, suffice it to say that you're on your way to developing a new set of skills (or behaviors) that will be sure to build and strengthen your emotional muscles!

FURTHER EXPLORATION

1. What do you think makes the connection between food and feeling so strong for you?

____

____

____

2. How did your childhood experiences reinforce focusing on eating or not eating when you're emotionally uncomfortable?

____

____

____

3. Why is food even more comforting when you're upset?

____

____

____

4. Why might you turn away from hunger and cravings rather than nourish yourself?

____

____

____

5. How would you describe the difference between how disordered and "normal" eaters use food when they're upset?

____

____

____

6. As you contemplate the idea of listening to both your feelings and your hunger, what inner tugs of resistance do you notice?

____

____

____

____

7. How do you feel about overcoming your emotional connection to food: hopeful, hopeless, or mixed?

____

____

____

8. In general, how would you rate your connection to your feelings: strong, moderate, poor, non-existent?

____

____

____

9. What do you need to do to increase your connection to your emotions?

____

____

____

____

10. How can you improve at tuning into physical sensations that may be pre-cursors to emotions?

____

____

____

11. Where do you imagine you are in the process of breaking the connection between food and feelings? Do you feel as if you're taking your first step? Do you think you may be halfway there?

____

____

____

4

The Seven Most Difficult Feelings for Disordered Eaters

(More Like Seven Hundred!)

I hope you didn't read the title of this chapter and think, "What? Only *seven* difficult feelings? They're *all* difficult for me." Take heart, you're not alone; many people feel exactly as you do. But remember, everyone's got to start somewhere, and you're taking a giant step forward by reading this workbook. Believe me, if you can learn to handle these seven emotions—guilt, shame, anxiety, helplessness, disappointment, confusion, and loneliness—you'll be well prepared for whatever comes your way.

Are there really only seven difficult feelings?

When I started to research the subject of feelings, I found extensive disagreement about what constitutes human emotion. One expert maintained that surprise, joy, interest, rage, disgust, shame, fear, and anguish are the only emotions hard-wired into us. Another claimed that only surprise, anger, fear, happiness, disgust, and sadness are innate. Yet a third argued that the four basic emotional response patterns are panic, rage, expectancy, and fear. So much for research!

Instead, I turned to my decades of professional experience counseling and teaching overeaters and undereaters. Reflecting upon the kinds of distress, which debilitated my clients and students, led me to two observations. First, they regularly avoided or minimized a specific set of emotions. Second, it was these exact feelings, more often than not, that triggered acting out around food. This lead me to surmise that if people with eating problems could learn to effectively handle their most troubling emotions, it would significantly improve their relationship with food *and* enhance their emotional health.

Does everyone experience painful feelings the same way?

The short answer to this question is no. The subject is complex and must take into account both the feeling at hand and the individual's tolerance for pain. We can understand this dynamic better by viewing painful feelings as internal wounds that are much like external, physical wounds. Assessing both kinds of pain, we might consider similar factors—the site, size, nature, and depth of the wound, the person's general frame of mind, how they feel about the particular pain, whether or not they're suffering with other hurt, their ability to tolerate pain, and their previous experience with it.

Let's take these factors one by one and see if the process informs your understanding of painful emotions. The first factor is the nature and depth of wounding or pain. You'd probably agree that a slight insult, say, not being on the list for a dinner party hosted by someone you met once doesn't hurt nearly as much as not being invited to a close friend's wedding. The closer you are to people and the more you expect of them, the higher the likelihood of feeling zinged. By the same token, if your sister forgets to call you back because she's feeding her new baby, you probably won't get too bent out of shape. But if she neglects to stop by when you're in the hospital having a triple bypass, you'll likely be terribly offended. The point is that the nature and depth of emotional wounding are relevant predictors of how badly you may feel.

Next let's take your general frame of mind. If you're an upbeat person for whom the glass is usually half full, you'll have an easier time with emotional pain than if you're a gloom-and-doomer who'd bemoan the one cloud in an otherwise magnificent blue sky. If you're a positive individual, even when your feelings get hurt, you might think the wounding is unintentional and let it go. However, if you're a pessimist, tend to personalize, or see yourself as a perpetual victim, you'll zero right in on the pain, making it loom larger than it really is. Also, if you're the upbeat type, your spirits will bounce back to normal far more quickly after a perceived injury than someone who believes they live under a black cloud. Some people simply have more buoyancy and emotional resilience than others.

Your mindset also makes a difference. If you're convinced that you can't deal with rejection and just *know* you'll be marooned on bummer-island for the rest of your life if you don't get the job you want, you're setting yourself up for misery. If, on the other hand, rejection doesn't bother you as much as, say, guilt, you'll be able to neutralize the sting and move on. It's all in your perspective, the frame you place around the picture.

Along with your general state of mind, it's important to consider whether you're suffering from one emotional wound or a host of them. For instance, if your best friend moves away a week after your house burns down and your dog is put to sleep, you might understandably feel emotionally overwhelmed and that you're about to lose your mind. On the other hand, if your wife walks out but you have a terrific job and a troupe of supportive family and friends, you might believe you'll make it through the night. But, remember, even emotionally strong and resourceful people may go under temporarily when everything goes wrong at once.

Now let's look at a person's ability to tolerate pain. This subject has been researched a good deal and scientific studies conclude that tolerance for both physical and emotional pain depends in large part on an individual's biochemical makeup (that is, their brain chemistry). Deficits in natural pain soothers such as serotonin, for example, make you more prone toward depression and anxiety than people who possess a normal quantity. Moreover, if your experience has proved you can handle pain, your expectation will be positive—and vice versa. If you're a person with low pain tolerance, the slightest insult may feel devastating, whereas if you're a person with high pain tolerance, you may be able to shrug it off.

Lastly, let's explore how your history of emotional wounding might affect how you deal with painful feelings. If you've been the victim of severe abuse and/or neglect or have suffered other trauma, you will almost certainly be a good deal more sensitive to emotional wounding than other people (even if you don't realize it). Unfortunately, along with an increased sensitivity, you also might have a decreased physiological capacity to tolerate suffering because regular and excessive stress can severely deplete the production of neurotransmitters that regulate emotions. Moreover, years of suffering may have heightened your despair and diminished your hope. You may possess little reserve for comforting or taking care of yourself. Tending to your wounds may be too hard, particularly when old wounds haven't healed before you've suffered new ones.

We can't help comparing ourselves to other people even when we try to resist. Making comparisons in the area of emotional pain are particularly tricky. If you and your friend burn yourselves while taking a glass-blowing class, you can inspect and compare wounds. But when you tell a friend you're severely depressed and he says he is too, you're moving from the concrete to the abstract. Do you both experience exactly the same sensations when you're blue? How do you measure your pain against your friend's? Is yours as bad or worse than his?

Everyone's pain is subjective, whether physical or emotional.

What's unbearable for you may be tolerable for someone else or the other way around. In trying to comprehend why people experience emotional wounding differently, it's important not to make judgments or compare yourself with others in a way that makes you feel inadequate or a failure. *Remember that everyone starts out at a different place and we are all limited, in part, by genetics and our early life.* Although all emotional pain has elements in common, everyone's heartache is unique.

✓ STOP AND FEEL

How do you feel about your ability to tolerate emotional wounding?

____

____

____

☼ PRACTICE EXERCISE

Identifying Feelings

PURPOSE: To learn to identify feelings

RATIONALE: Effective handling of feelings starts with recognizing an emotion and labeling it correctly, with a goal of becoming as familiar with your emotions as you are with your senses.

WHAT YOU NEED: pen

DIRECTIONS: This exercise has two parts. First, write your own take on guilt, shame, anxiety, helplessness, disappointment, confusion, and loneliness.

Guilt

____

____

Shame

____

____

Anxiety

____

____

Helplessness

____

____

Disappointment

____

____

Confusion

____

____

Loneliness

____

____

Second, write down all the situations that trigger each emotion. Take your time in your descriptions and in visualizing the circumstance that provoke distress.

Triggers to guilt

____

____

Triggers to shame

____

____

Triggers to anxiety

____

____

Triggers to helplessness

____

____

Triggers to disappointment

____

____

Triggers to confusion

____

____

Triggers to loneliness

____

____

REFLECTION (to be done after completion of exercise): Was it hard or easy to describe these emotions? Did it make you uncomfortable even thinking about them? What did you learn about the situations that make you affectively uncomfortable? Did you have many triggers or only a few?

____

____

____

> *Why are guilt, shame, anxiety, helplessness, disappointment, confusion, and loneliness the most difficult feelings for disordered eaters?*

The seven emotions I've chosen may or may not resonate with you and that's fine. If you've been working on emotional healing for a long time, you may find only one or two feelings truly vexing. However, if you're a novice, don't despair. In the following pages of this book, you'll find a chapter devoted exclusively to each emotion I've chosen, but for now, let me briefly explain my selections.

I chose ***Guilt*** because it's so pervasive in our society and even more so in the lives of the people I counsel and teach. Practically every dysfunctional eater I've come across is other-oriented, a caretaker, a do-gooder, has an overly-developed sense of responsibility, and rarely (if ever) believes she is doing enough. Every failed relationship is *her* fault, every situation that needs fixing is *her* job, every person with a problem becomes *her* pet project. Many clients live in a constant state of guilt, as if they can never get things right or do as much as they believe they should. They have such incredibly high standards for themselves that they're doomed to fall short. Because they're often people-pleasers and feel naughty and selfish when they do things for themselves, their self-care is only fair to poor. The major way they take care of themselves is—you guessed it—through food.

Shame was a natural choice because disordered eaters live so far outside a state of grace. Most of my clients are convinced that their behavior is sinful and disgusting, but nevertheless, are unable or unwilling to stop. This makes me wonder whether shame isn't part of the unconscious attraction of having an eating problem. Nine out of ten times, these clients come from shame-based families and the feeling is strongly familiar to them. One of the ways they express this feeling is through food addiction and obsession, and attaining a weight that is grossly below or above the norm. Disordered eating may be a way to maintain the shame they unconsciously think they ought to feel or are used to feeling.

At the rock bottom of all of our emotional suffering is ***helplessness***, which occurs when there's nothing we can do. It underlies many feelings—frustration, impatience, anger, and anxiety. We can't help but feel its reverberations from infancy and childhood. Although we may not recall lying powerless in the crib, our bodies hold the memories. In the later years of childhood and adulthood, feeling helpless is often associated with fear that something bad will happen, a double whammy—*something terrible is going to happen and I can't do a damned thing about it.* Many disordered eaters combat their helplessness by taking action, usually in the form of micromanaging their food intake or consuming every morsel in sight.

I chose ***anxiety*** because a significant number of my clients eat to soothe their nerves. Many have a family history of depression or anxiety and may lack the proper balance of neurotransmitters to help them relax. These individuals are anxious about what they did yesterday and about what they're going to do tomorrow. It's hard for them to stay in the moment and shut off shoulda-woulda-coulda judgments. The activities that often soothe them, though only temporarily, revolve around food or involve control over their appetite. Of course, eating and weight may then become additional things about which to be anxious.

Disappointment lends itself so easily to acting out with food that it's surprising that everyone doesn't turn to it when they feel let down. Chronic disappointment can lead people to believe that they don't deserve to have positive expectations and outcomes in life. Wanting causes them to feel needy and so they deny their genuine desires. Because it's too scary to have expectations of themselves or of other people, they turn to something that's predictable and always in good supply—food. When an emotional eater suffers the letdown of disappointment, food picks them up, at least for a while. The restrictive eater often deals with disappointment by actually raising their expectations of themselves by obsessive calorie counting and fixating on thinness, as if to say, "Others might disappoint me, but I have high standards. Thin will never disappointment me."

Confusion is often overlooked as a troubling emotion because it's considered one of the "smaller" feelings, not a giant like fear or shame. But it runs rampant in a population of eaters who are out of touch with their physical needs and wants. They're not sure whether they're really hungry or deserve to eat, what they should eat, when they're full, what they ought to look like, and what they should weigh. Most of their confusion is about the concept of *enough* in numerous areas of their lives. What drives their confusion is the desperate urge to find out what's right so they won't fail or make mistakes. Because it's difficult to tolerate the tension created by vague, mixed or conflicting feelings, they often give up and instead take a stroll down a supermarket aisle or focus on numbers, which are sharp and clear—on a scale or food package.

Loneliness is such a soul killer that I'm not surprised that lonely people seek solace in food. To feel lonely harkens back to childhood fears of being abandoned, rejected, dismissed, ignored, unseen, and unheard. In our untutored young minds, when we weren't reflected in someone's eyes, we felt disconnected, invisible, and annihilated, as if we didn't exist. When disordered eaters feel this depth of loneliness, they're desperate to bond with something, *anything*—to merely feel alive. For some, eating reminds them of the comfort of being held and fed, connected to someone, and to a time when they were loved and valued. Others quell the emptiness and aloneness with obsessing about things they *can* control such as their food intake or weight and proving how little they need.

✓ STOP AND FEEL

What are you feeling right now?

____

____

____

☼ PRACTICE EXERCISE

Deep Breathing

PURPOSE: To use your breath to relax

RATIONALE: This is a great technique that you can do anywhere, any time to relax and center yourself. The more you practice, the more quickly your body will respond.

WHAT YOU NEED: chair, bed, or rug

DIRECTIONS: Get in a comfortable position, preferably sitting or laying down. Pay attention to your breathing and slow it down by inhaling to a count of five, and exhaling to a count of five. Then stretch it out to a count of six, inhaling and exhaling, then seven, then eight, and then reverse back to seven, six, and end with five. Focus on emptying your body of breath and tension and taking in new healing air. When thoughts pop up, observe them or gently push them away and return to counting and breathing. Do this exercise for at least five minutes or until you feel relaxed.

REFLECTION (to be done after completion of exercise): Did you notice a difference between how you felt before and after the exercise? Was it hard to quiet your mind and concentrate on your breath? Think of how slipping into a relaxed breathing mode when you're tense could be a great replacement for focusing on food.

____

____

____

Practice, practice, practice

Now I'm going to remind you of something you probably already know, but that you might need to hear again: you're not going to overcome your eating disorder *simply because you want to.* Intent is fine and dandy, but it *must* be coupled with consistent action for you to change. Happiness and emotional well-being will not descend upon you from on high just because you deserve good things in life.

> *Everyone deserves the best, but only the people who work hard at self-growth and self-transformation get it.*

You will begin to realize *your* dreams when you allow your emotions to speak to you, when you listen carefully to what they have to say, and when you make conscious choices based on authentic feelings coupled with sound judgment. To do this, however, you must become conversant with the language that emotions speak—and that's often the language of pain.

People who allow themselves to experience their heartache and learn from it lead happy, successful lives, whereas people who run from emotional pain end up unhappy and unfulfilled. Which kind of person do you want to be?

✓ STOP AND FEEL

Are you eager to read more about specific emotions, do you need a break, or do you feel an internal tug to give up?

____

____

____

FURTHER EXPLORATION

1. What three factors most affect your inability to experience and bear your feelings (e.g., early trauma, low pain tolerance, expect to have no pain, negative thinking)?

____

____

____

2. If you suffered neglect or emotional, physical, verbal, or sexual abuse as a child, how might that impact your ability to bear emotional pain now?

____

____

____

3. Are you generally an upbeat or downbeat person? How does your outlook affect your willingness to experience painful feelings?

____

____

____

4. If you handle any feelings effectively and appropriately, what can you learn from this experience that you can apply to other feelings?

____

____

____

5. What emotions trouble you the most?

____

____

____

6. In what ways, besides disordered eating, do you manage your feelings now? Are your methods effective or ineffective?

____

____

____

7. How are you feeling right now about learning more about feelings?

____

____

____

5

Guilt

(It's a Feeling, Not a Permanent Medical Condition!)

Funny as it may seem that anyone could confuse an emotion with an illness, there's nothing humorous about guilt. The fact is that chronic or frequent guilt feels like having a low-grade virus. You never know when it's going to flare up or how long you'll be incapacitated, but you know for sure it's going to be a punishing experience. If you've ever been wracked with guilt, you know the comparison to a virus is on the mark. Think about it. When a virus attacks your computer, it's said to corrupt it or "infect it with errors." Isn't that exactly how you feel when you're guilty?

Guilt is associated with fewer physical sensations than some other emotions, like fear, anger, or helplessness, but it's hardly a subtle fellow; far from it, it's pushy and a bit of a pest. When you feel guilty, it's as if something is hanging over you, hovering around, or gnawing at you from the inside. Guilt is the nag that won't let you forget what you did, the pebble that keeps pressing itself onto your psyche and won't let you move on, the thorn in your side that keeps needling you about what you did wrong. It can be sharp and quick, a knife of an emotion—*I meant to call Uncle George when he was in the hospital, I need to pay those bills, how could I have spent the day watching TV when I have so much to do, how could I have said such awful things to my father.* Guilt can also worm its way into your soul, kick off its shoes and settle in, robbing you of your self-worth and causing you to feel as if your life is one long apology.

What is the purpose of guilt?

Although it may seem like a pathological state, guilt is a tremendously useful and compelling tool whose simple purpose is to teach us right from wrong. Guilt flags behavior that fails to meet our internal standard or self-expectation, what psychology calls an *ego ideal*. Even though it often feels as if it comes from without, guilt rises from within. It springs from the place that wishes to be perfect or a good deal closer to it than we'll ever be. It arises from what is noblest and finest in us, from our highest aspirations, our purest moral self. Guilt tells us that we've transgressed according to our personal commandments.

The capacity to feel guilt helps us monitor our behavior and treat others as we wish to be treated. Without it, we'd have no sense of right or wrong and society would be a chaotic free-for-all (more so than it is already!). A world without guilt would be like driving on a complicated, convoluted highway system with no red lights or traffic signs. People would zoom around with no restraint or regard for others or for the rules of the road. In a guilt-free society, the end would always justify the means, there'd be no doubts or second thoughts, and fairness, justice, and decency would fly out the window. Who'd want to live in that kind of uncivilized society?

Guilt is the mechanism that keeps us in line and enables us to live harmoniously in community. When we step out of bounds, bounds *we've* established, we feel badly and try not to repeat the action because we know that if we do, we'll feel guilty all over again. You may not have thought so before, but guilt is a necessity, an essential emotion, a laudable and practical way to keep ourselves in check. Think of it as the internal ruler that makes sure we measure up to our own standards.

✓ STOP AND FEEL

How do you feel about the time you spend feeling guilty?

____

____

____

☼ PRACTICE EXERCISE

Trip Up Your Guilt

PURPOSE: To stop guilt tripping yourself

RATIONALE: Too many of us hold onto guilt for too long. Applying rational thinking to guilt will help you let go of it and move on.

WHAT YOU NEED: memories

DIRECTIONS: Think of a situation (current, recent, or ancient) that has caused you a good deal of guilt. By calling up the gory details, allow yourself to re-experience your remorse or regret to the max. Sit with the feeling until you're immersed in it. Now come up with one just reason to feel less guilty about the situation (maybe you've taken steps to make amends or have already been forgiven).

Reason 1

____

____

____

Now that you've got one reason, come up with two more.

Reason 2

____

____

____

Reason 3

____

____

____

Now that you have three reasons, see if you can drum up a final reason not to feel guilty at all.

Reason 4

____

____

____

REFLECTION (to be done after completion of exercise): Were you able to shed your guilt? How does that feel? Notice how you can overcome guilt by rationality. What are you afraid of in letting go of feeling guilty?

____

____

____

Can people make me feel guilty?

No, no, and no again. Get my point? Although you may insist that someone "made you feel guilty," it's not possible. *No one can make another person feel guilt or any other emotion.* Feelings arise from within, not without. If humans could make each other feel specific emotions, I'd be first in line to make everyone feel great about themselves and go off to play shuffleboard. What you generally mean when you say that someone "made" you feel guilt (or any emotion) is that some verbal or non-verbal behavior of theirs stirred up a feeling that you did something unacceptable or wrong—and now you feel badly about it. That is, your reaction (conscious or unconscious, intentional or unintentional) to the person or situation was that you didn't measure up to an internal standard or expectation. The truth is that you might have a variety of reactions to their guilt-tripping, other than guilt—repulsion, amusement, rage, curiosity—or none at all. No one *causes* your feelings; you *cause* your feelings.

No one can make another person feel guilt or any other emotion.

Let me clarify. You'll only feel guilty if your internal standard and the external one by which you measure yourself are the same. Here's an illustration of how the process works. When I receive dozens of year-end solicitations from charities, I sorely wish that I could give to every worthy cause. Each request tries to convince me that the right thing to do is to take some money from my pocket and put it into theirs. The subtle or not-so-subtle implication is that if I don't donate to them, I'm doing something wrong. All of them, of course, are trying to whip up my guilt so that I'll write a fat check. If *I* also feel that I should respond to every request that crosses my desk and that I should never refuse anyone in need, I won't help but feel guilty. However, I know that if I give to every charity that solicits me, I'll end up broke and pretty soon someone will have to create a charity to support me!

If I feel guilty in this circumstance, it's because *I* didn't live up to my own standard which is the same as that of the charity—that I should give because they're deserving. On the other hand, let's say that I don't give a hoot about anyone but myself. I could receive hundreds of solicitations and be spared feeling the teensiest pinch of guilt. Why? Because my higher self or ego ideal would fail to place value on giving to those in need. I might think, *let them fend for themselves, no one ever gave me a nickel so why should I help someone else. They'll only waste the money anyway,* or *I wish they'd stop being such a nuisance.* Absent the perception of myself as a kind, charitable person, I'd have no cause to experience guilt.

Here's another example. Let's say your mother insists that you visit her on Saturday morning, but you're dying for a workout. Do you *have to* feel guilty if you pass on seeing her and head for the gym? You might think so. In fact, as my client, you might try your darndest to convince me that you *had* to go see her and skip your workout because she'd do such a guilt trip on you. And I'd come right back by challenging your thinking and explaining that no one can make you feel anything. People can make you do things you don't want to do, but how can they make or cause you to have a specific mental or emotional reaction? Your mother may try her utmost to trigger your guilt, but can she really crawl inside of you and manipulate your feelings? Preposterous!

Try this one on for size. During the Sixties, there was a great deal of so-called counter-culture activity across the country and around the globe—demonstrations, sit-ins, marches, rallies, and street theatre. The "Establishment" believed that these activities threatened civilization as they knew it and tried to ban or stop the protests. But the demonstrators insisted that they were putting themselves on the line for what they believed was right. Could the Establishment have made the demonstrators feel guilty for their rebellious actions? No way, because the demonstrators had a different set of expectations and ideals for themselves than the Establishment had for them. Now this doesn't mean that decades later, some former dissidents didn't modify their values and feel guilty about the damage or harm they'd caused way back when. The point is that guilt can only be produced when a person isn't meeting his or her own moral standards.

✓ *STOP AND FEEL*

What are you feeling right now?

____

____

____

Does everyone feel guilt?

Yes, everyone feels guilt, to a greater or lesser extent. But because guilt arises fairly spontaneously when we fail to meet our own standards, people who have high expectations for themselves suffer more guilt than people who have low expectations. Not surprisingly, perfectionists suffer from practically perpetual guilt. Their self-imposed standards are so (unrealistically) high that they can't possibly maintain them. Instead of lowering their expectations, though, they strain and strain for the gold ring that will always be out of reach.

At the other end of the spectrum, selfish, self-centered, self-absorbed people—called narcissists—may rarely suffer authentic guilt because, although they may have ridiculously high expectations of others, their standards for their own behaviors are often shockingly low. I'm not saying that you should aspire to be selfish merely to avoid feeling guilty. Believe me, narcissists are far from happy people. Though at times they may appear to feel guilty, what they experience may not spring from a genuine sense of having done wrong but from a need to manipulate others' feelings and behavior.

Additionally, people with what is called Antisocial Personality Disorder appear to feel minimal, if any, guilt in situations that would trigger it in most people. We used to label such individuals, who could commit heinous crimes and exhibit no regret or remorse, as *sociopaths*. For them, the end *does* justify the means. They're fascinating characters in a creepy way when we see them in movies or TV, but unsettling and terrifying to be around in real life. It's likely that Antisocial Personality Disorder is rooted in a person's biology (genetics and biochemistry), psychology, and social history.

Both narcissistic and anti-social individuals lack a strong capacity for empathy—the ability to put one's self in another's place—which is the cornerstone of guilt. Think of empathy as the key to harmonious community relations. If you can't imagine how someone feels, you can't imagine his or her hurt. And if you can't imagine their hurt, you may neither recognize nor care that you caused it. Fortunately for society, most of us have a functioning conscience—and some of us have too much of a good thing!

☼ PRACTICE EXERCISE

Guilt Trip Odometer

PURPOSE: To increase awareness of feeling guilty and the ability to distinguish between valid and automatic, invalid guilt

RATIONALE: It's as crucial to not feel guilt when you've done nothing wrong, as it is to feel it when you have. Letting go of guilt that isn't yours will lighten your load and make bearing it easier when it's justified.

WHAT YOU NEED: memories

DIRECTIONS: Pretend you're wearing an odometer that registers guilt, a highly sensitive instrument that records every instance, day in and day out. If you were to take a reading off your guilt-o-meter right now, how many times would it indicate that you felt guilty today? _____ Yesterday? _____ This week? _____ Try and recall each instance and decide whether your guilt was automatic and invalid or justifiable because you did something you truly regret.

Incident 1 ____

Justified?_____ Unjustified?_____

Incident 2 ____

Justified?_____ Unjustified?_____

Incident 3 ____

Justified?_____ Unjustified?_____

REFLECTION (to be done after completion of exercise): What did you learn about how you view guilt? Were there any surprises? Guilt can become a habit like any other, so be wary and flip on your awareness switch whenever it tugs at your heart.

____

____

____

How did I learn about guilt?

Guilt has the potential to show up on the scene when you develop a conscience at about five or six years old. If you're a two-year-old romping around your living room and toss Daddy's brand new Rolex into the fireplace, you won't feel guilty. You'll undoubtedly feel upset when Daddy reprimands you to never, ever do that again, but you won't feel guilt because you've yet to develop the internal capacity to know right from wrong. You'll only feel badly because someone you love very much is angry with you. If, however, as a seven year old with a developing conscience, you fling Daddy's watch into the fire while horsing around, you'll (hopefully) be aware that you've done something you shouldn't.

There are many physiological changes that your brain undergoes before it reaches maturity between the ages of 20 and 30. For a young child, possessing the psychological structures for what we call a *conscience* and the ability to feel guilt are major developmental milestones. Although today we have nursery and pre-school for toddlers, there was a time when children weren't allowed to enter school until they were five or six years old precisely because the attainment of a conscience was a prerequisite for them to function appropriately and compatibly in a group. It's no accident that formal schooling begins at the time that conscience is forming.

The development of a conscience is both a biological and social phenomenon. Your physiology builds the mental and emotional structures in your brain that support a conscience, what some in psychology call a *superego*, and your parents and caretakers hopefully take advantage of this achievement to teach you right from wrong. They do this in two ways. They model behavior—by, say, returning a wallet someone has dropped, apologizing for hurting a person's feelings, and telling the truth when they've done something wrong. They also let you know what's right and wrong by how they react to you. To put it in simple behavioral terms, they reward or give you positive reinforcement when you do something they believe to be right, and punish or provide negative reinforcement when you do something they believe to be wrong.

In essence, they show you how your conscience operates by modeling how theirs works and by giving you the guidance to get yours up and running. When you receive reinforcement for telling the truth, being kind to others, taking responsibility for your mistakes, and apologizing when you do something wrong, your conscience is being primed in the hopes that it will work automatically as you grow and mature. I remember years ago watching a friend and his five-year-old in fascination. Before leaving the room, the father had warned his son not to touch the TV. After his father left, the boy stood in front of the screen, shaking his head from side to side, forcefully saying "No" to himself over and over. This is how conscience develops, through mimicry—and where there's conscience, the potential for guilt exists.

Reinforcement works on two levels, the concrete and the emotional. For example, let's say as a young girl you pinch your sister and she begins to cry. After explaining that pinching your sister is a hurtful and unacceptable behavior, your parents give you a time-out in your room. The punishment affects you in two ways: You feel unhappy and uncomfortable that you displeased your parents whom you love (emotional level) and you're not crazy about being banished to your room either, even for a short period of time (concrete level).

Or, let's say you're a thirteen-year-old jock playing touch football with your buddies, and your neighbor with Down's syndrome who's about your age, wants to join the fun. He's basically a good egg and not even a bad receiver. Your friends reject the idea, but you insist that they let him join you. He ends up playing surprisingly well and when your parents find out that you stood up for him, they offer to take you to the movies for such a gracious act. Again, notice how the reward works on two levels: You feel terrific that your parents are proud of you (emotional level), as well as getting to enjoy a movie (concrete level).

As you can see, there are powerful reinforcers to help you learn right from wrong—concrete rewards and punishments that elicit negative or positive emotions in you. When all goes well, your parents model moral behavior *for* you and reinforce it *in* you, and you receive a clear message of what is wrong and right. In an age-appropriate way, they help you develop your own moral values by encouraging you to grapple with ethical decisions and reflect on your behavior and choices.

> *Emotionally healthy parents recognize both that they have to give you guidance, and that you must make your own mistakes and live with the consequences of your actions.*

Often the guilt that is most obvious is what you feel *about* your actions—when you've let yourself or someone else down. However, you may also learn in childhood to suffer guilt over what you feel—a secondary emotion. If, for example, as a teenager, you planned to attend a concert with your friends but were coerced into baby-sitting for your younger brother because your parents wanted to go out, you might have felt justifiably disappointed and angry. If you expressed those feelings, even appropriately, and your parents insisted, "You shouldn't feel that way," or tried to guilt-trip you, you may have felt you were a bad person for your feelings. What you learned from their reaction was that there are emotions—in this case, disappointment and anger—that are not okay to feel, and certainly not acceptable to express.

Although your disappointment and anger may have been appropriate, you were erroneously instructed that what you felt was wrong, which led you to believe—also erroneously—that the feeling was wrong. You may understand now that it was your parents who should have felt guilty for keeping you home after promising you could go to the concert, but that doesn't change the lesson that stuck. If your parents regularly chastised you for having negative feelings in response to abridgement of your rights and denial of your needs, you probably learned that rather than feel angry, it was more comfortable to feel guilty. You may have learned that feeling any sort of entitlement to happiness was unacceptable and now, every time you assert your rights and needs, you feel guilty instead.

✓ STOP AND FEEL

How do you feel about what you learned about guilt from your parents?

____

____

____

BELIEFS ABOUT GUILT

Because rational thinking leads to rational behavior, it's essential that you build a belief-system that's sound and healthy. Here are examples of irrational thoughts about guilt turned into rational ones.

IB: People can make me feel guilty.
RB: No one can make me feel guilty.
Only I can make myself feel guilty.

IB: If I feel guilty it means I've done something wrong.
RB: If I feel guilty it means I need to reflect on whether I've done something wrong.

IB: Feeling guilty means I'm a bad person.
RB: Feeling guilty means I may have done something that doesn't meet my standards.

IB: I can't bear feeling guilty.
RB: I can bear feeling guilty and any other feeling I have.

IB: If I've done something wrong, I should feel guilty.
RB: If I've done something wrong, I need to reflect on my behavior but not necessarily feel guilty.

IB: I should feel guilty if I undereat or overeat.
RB: I need to understand why I undereat or overeat, but I don't have to feel guilty.

IB: If I felt guilt more often about my eating, I'd eat better.
RB: I can improve my relationship with food without feeling guilty about it.

IB: I should feel guilty about my weight.
RB: I can accept myself at any weight and have no guilt about it.

Now it's your turn to transform your dysfunctional beliefs into sound, functional ones. Take your time and make sure that each new, rational belief feels right for you. They should be concrete and written in the present tense using an active verb. Feel free to use the list above, but make sure you come up with some of your own as well.

Irrational Belief	**Rational Belief**
______________________	______________________
______________________	______________________
______________________	______________________
______________________	______________________

Can I have too much guilt?

Unfortunately, yes, you can end up feeling guilt-ridden practically all of the time, which can be incapacitating and destroy the quality of your life. If you feel chronically guilty—that you're to blame for most things that go wrong in your life (or anyone else's!)—your conscience is in overdrive. While it's appropriate and healthy to take responsibility for genuine mistakes and failures, it's inappropriate and unhealthy to feel guilty when you have done nothing wrong.

It's inappropriate and unhealthy to feel guilty when you have done nothing wrong.

You may suffer from chronic, unhealthy guilt if you always say you're sorry even when it's unwarranted, if you apologize profusely beyond what's necessary or appropriate for your transgressions, if you generally assume that you're wrong and the other person is right, or if you consistently berate yourself for real or imagined wrongdoings. Perhaps a hefty dose of religious training while growing up has caused you to mistakenly believe you should be punished for your sins and that guilt and suffering are a normal and natural way of life. Well, they're not!

Somewhere along the line you may have learned you're responsible for the well-being of others. Maybe you had to look after a brood of brothers and sisters while your parents worked. Or perhaps one of your parents (or a sibling) was physically or mentally ill and tending to them was your responsibility. It could be that one or both of your parents suffered from drug abuse or alcoholism, and you were the only responsible person in the household, even at a (too) young age.

Or you may be used to assuming things are your fault because your parents had difficulty taking responsibility for their actions and habitually blamed you instead. When you're a little person and they're big and powerful (and you're dependent upon them), you had little choice but to believe them. Unfortunately, children are perfect scapegoats for parents who refuse to acknowledge their mistakes.

Healthy guilt motivates you to reflect on and assess your behavior according to your (hopefully reasonable) moral standards. You can do this prior to or after making a choice. If you're thinking about taking an action, say, refusing a request to take your friend to the airport at six a.m. on your day off, you need to consider whether you'll feel guilty if you say no. If you imagine you will, you might lean toward making the trip. Or, you may decide that you'll feel just fine suggesting he take a cab.

Alternatively, you may not have a chance to reflect beforehand, but refuse your friend's request and end up thinking about it afterward. Then you may or may not feel guilty according to a number of factors, including what you've done for him in the past and what he's done for you, the general quality of your friendship, whether there's anyone else who could take him, how badly you want or need to sleep in, and so forth.

When you experience unhealthy guilt, you automatically feel guilty whenever you take care of your own needs and say "No" to someone else's. You don't take into account whether someone's request is reasonable, appropriate, or fair. You say "Yes" *because* you're afraid of feeling guilty. But guilt isn't meant to function as an automatic response to behavior. If you feel chronic guilt, you've acquired a rotten habit of assuming that you're always wrong and others are always right. Perhaps it's time to consider that other people might be the ones who are behaving badly!

The way to use guilt in a healthy manner is to reflect on a situation, and if you determine that you're genuinely at fault, make amends if possible, and then decide how you can do things differently in the future. That's it. Once you've used guilt to figure out that you've made a mistake and how to correct it, you've reached your stop and it's time to get off the guilt train—the feeling has served its purpose. There is absolutely no good reason to remain on that train once you've realized the error of your ways.

✓ STOP AND FEEL

How do you feel about giving up chronic guilt and holding other people responsible for what they do and say?

____

____

____

Is there a correlation between feeling guilty and my issues with food and weight?

Suffering from chronic or inappropriate guilt and having eating problems have a few things in common. Underlying both is an uncertainty about how much is enough. With food, it's waffling about the right amount to eat to be fit, healthy, and maintain a comfortable weight. With guilt, it's wondering how much to do to be a "good" person. Both involve seeking a balance between saying "Yes" and "No" to yourself and others, trusting your own judgment, and utilizing effective self-regulation skills.

How well you determine sufficiency—in terms of giving to others, taking responsibility, and especially in the realm of food and weight—depends primarily upon how well your early caretakers reinforced what you felt was right for you. If you were a picky, small eater whose parents made you finish every last morsel even if it made you uncomfortable, you may have felt guilty leaving food and not living up to their expectations. Now, when you fail to clean your plate, you react as if you're doing something wrong. Or if you had a large appetite and there wasn't enough food to go around for the family, you may have believed you were a glutton and felt guilty wanting more. Today, you identify wanting food or more food with being too needy or greedy.

Repeated denials of your authentic feelings eventually eroded your self-trust and self-confidence, setting the stage for you now, as an adult, to doubt your own responses with food, and often, everything else. Today, rather than use intuition and judgment to recognize and monitor what is enough, you use guilt. For example, say your father often made fun of you for still being hungry after dinner. As an adult, you might deny hunger and craving to silence the inner voice that insists you're not entitled to eat and should feel badly if you do. Alternately, you may feel guilty saying "No" to food because, as a child, you couldn't say "I'm full or satisfied" without your mother getting upset and blaming you for all the hours she slaved in the kitchen. Now you feel unbearable guilt (and anxiety) when you don't eat everything that's put in front of you.

The only way to overcome guilt connected to food and to improve your "felt" sense of what is enough is to change your beliefs about your ability to recognize sufficiency and to practice saying "Yes" and "No" in the right balance for you.

> *You need to work on two fronts simultaneously: identifying what is enough and letting go of inappropriate guilt.*

Try reframing your beliefs about self-trust and self-knowledge. Practice asking yourself what's enough in various situations (food or otherwise), and refuse to feel guilty as long as you're acting on authentic feelings or body signals.

Guilt is connected to disordered eating in another way, which relates to how you take care of yourself. Perhaps when you were young, your parents failed to adequately meet your emotional and physical needs—for help, stimulation, guidance, comfort, or pleasure. You might have turned to food because it made you feel better without generating feelings of guilt and neediness. It was your attempt to take care of yourself the best way you knew how. Or you felt naughty eating, but did it anyway because it provoked *less* guilt than wanting other things. Even today you'd rather feel guilty about food than about going after what you really yearn for in life: love, attention, affection, time alone, a vacation, or someone to take care of you.

If you want to disconnect feeling guilty from food, you have to find better ways to take care of yourself. You'll also need to refuse to feel guilty the times that you still turn to or away from eating when you're emotionally distressed. This means taking risks to discover what you really need to live a fulfilling life and feeling entitled to all that your heart desires. Remember, you may initially feel guilty when you do something like say "Yes" to a "fattening" treat or tell your mom that you're not eating another bite. If so, you'll have to gently push away your guilt because you're not doing something wrong—you're doing something right.

You may also use disordered eating to punish yourself when you're feeling guilty. Maybe you believe you don't deserve food because it's too pleasurable and nourishing, or that being stuffed and nauseous is your just desserts for not being a saint. Let's return to a previous example of choosing a workout at the gym over paying a visit to your demanding mother to see how guilt insinuates itself into your relationship with food. You may feel like such a bad, ungrateful child that you return starving from your workout, but as punishment, won't allow yourself to eat. Or else you obsess about weight to distract yourself from your ugly feelings. Or you may feel like such a selfish witch for taking care of yourself instead of your mother that you raid your kitchen cabinets until nothing is left to eat.

Please remember that no matter how bad you think you are and how guilty you feel, you *always* deserve to eat if you're hungry. Always! Feeling good or bad about yourself has *nothing* to do with your body's need for nourishment. Your upbringing and early choices may have confused the two, but it's time to separate them for good. When you're feeling guilty, you need to examine whether or not you did something wrong. If so, take it from there and figure out what to do. If not, let the guilt go.

Whether you're an overeater or undereater, please remember that disordered eating is merely your misguided attempt to look after yourself and meet your emotional needs. If you were able to do this more effectively, you would. (And if you keep reading, you will be able to!) The goal is to stop feeling guilty and to start taking care of yourself more effectively.

FURTHER EXPLORATION

1. How do you know when you feel guilty (that is, what are the physical sensations)?

____

____

____

2. Is guilt an easy or difficult emotion for you to identify?

____

____

____

3. What purpose does guilt serve for you?

____

____

____

4. Why is it true that people cannot make you feel guilt (or any feeling)?

____

____

____

5. What did you learn about feeling guilty from your parents, including how they handled guilt and what they taught you about it by word or example?

____

____

____

6. What did you learn in school or through religious training about guilt?

____

____

____

7. What secondary feelings do you have about feeling guilty (i.e., shame, anger, etc.)?

____

____

____

8. Do you carry around too much guilt (hint: Do you apologize or say you're sorry automatically, fear, agonize about, or avoid hurting people's feelings, generally assume you're in the wrong, feel badly when you want or need things for yourself?)?

____

____

____

9. How do you focus on food or weight when you're feeling guilty?

____

____

____

10. What situations or people trigger your guilt?

____

____

____

11. What changes could you make right now to stop feeling unnecessary, excessive guilt?

____

____

____

6

Shame

(I'm Reading This Chapter Under the Covers!)

When it comes to emotions, shame is one of the big shots. There is nothing subtle or vague about it—it slams into you like a speeding locomotive. Shame is a ferocious, overwhelming, debilitating emotion that implies gravest wrongdoing and transgression beyond redemption. When you're ashamed, you want to vaporize your subhuman self on the spot, or at the very least, crawl under a rock and never come out.

Many people confuse shame with embarrassment and guilt, using the terms interchangeably. Unfortunately, this does justice to none of them. Think of shame, embarrassment, and guilt not as identical, but as distant cousins. Guilt, you may remember, is a failure to live up to your own standards. Embarrassment is a momentary awkwardness, self-consciousness, or uneasiness. Characterized by its transitory nature, it implies a gaff or goof, a lapse of judgment, a simple blunder, a *faux pas* you may be able to smile at down the road or perhaps even joke about with close friends.

Shame goes deeper—far deeper. You may eventually neutralize its sting, but it's doubtful that you'll ever have a giggle over whatever happened. More likely, you'll try to avoid public exposure of your act at all cost. In fact, because of its cringe potential, the word "shame" rarely crops up except in clinical circles. Colloquially, "I'm embarrassed" is often inaccurately substituted for "I'm ashamed" because it sounds (and feels) so much better. However, minimizing feelings for comfort's sake only promotes the false impression that they hold some sort of power over you. Name them exactly for what they are and *you* gain power over *them.*

How do I know if I'm feeling shame?

When you can't shake the feeling that you've done something horribly, unforgivably, unequivocally wrong, and that you are surely the worst person on earth because of it, shame is paying you a visit. You may flush deeply or feel any of the following: a prickly, hot sensation coursing through your extremities, sick to your stomach, or as if you've been punched in the solar plexis. You might feel repulsed by yourself—literally "sick of you." Shame is the stone in your gut that won't dissolve, striking at the very core of esteem, as you shudder, "*I* did *that*?" When you're ashamed, you feel dirty or soiled, as if no amount of washing could make you clean.

✓ STOP AND FEEL

How does the subject of shame make you uncomfortable?

____

____

____

☼ PRACTICE EXERCISE

Shame vs. Embarrassment

PURPOSE: To distinguish shame from embarrassment

RATIONALE: Shame is so often confused with embarrassment that it's vital to understand the difference.

WHAT YOU NEED: memories

DIRECTIONS: Think of an incident in which you considered yourself embarrassed. Reflecting on it, are you *sure* you felt embarrassment? Now think of a time when you felt deeply ashamed, and compare the two affects. Call them up in detail so that you can re-experience their differences. Now, move on to identify times you thought you were embarrassed when you were actually ashamed.

Embarrassing incident

____

____

____

How did you know you were embarrassed and not ashamed?

____

____

____

Shameful incident

____

____

____

How did you know you were ashamed and not embarrassed?

____

____

____

REFLECTION (to be done after completion of exercise): Could you distinguish shame from embarrassment or did they seem identical? If you had difficulty, try describing each emotion in your own words and repeat the exercise. Did merely evoking shame cause such discomfort that you had a hard time staying focused on it?

____

____

____

What's the difference between guilt and shame?

Much has been written about the similarities and differences between guilt and shame. It's said that guilt is about *what we do* and shame is about *who we are,* that guilt is wrong behavior and shame is a wrongness within us; that guilt is the perception that we've made a mistake or failed, while shame is the perception that we *are* mistakes or failures. Guilt presumes a wrong can be righted and offers an opportunity for redemption, prodding us to reach out, make amends, and set things straight. Think about how it lessens when, for instance, you call back your boss and offer to go into the office though you'd planned to work from home or when you run after a friend shouting, "I'm so sorry, I didn't mean it." Guilt offers the hope of undoing and forgiveness.

With shame, however, there is no hope, no brighter future: what's done is done. You feel as if you can never make things right no matter what you do. Unlike guilt, shame, doesn't come with an eraser.

✓ *STOP AND FEEL*

Does your discomfort with shame drive you to focus on food? Does your dysfunctional eating cause you shame?

____

____

____

What is the purpose of shame?

Shame stems from the belief that you have not merely done a bad thing, but that you are a bad person. Although it's hard to believe that an emotion so wounding and devastating has a purpose, it does. Precisely *because* of its potency, shame is a useful governing tool to prod you in what society perceives as the right direction. Like guilt, its essential purpose is to warn that you've missed the mark, fallen short of an expectation, stepped outside convention or the law, or behaved badly.

For example, if you promised to pick up your spouse's dry cleaning on the way home from work and it slipped your mind, you might feel a twinge of guilt. Reflecting a bit more, you might feel a stab of shame as you realize that your so-called forgetfulness stemmed from how angry you still are at your spouse from an argument you had the night before. You can let go of your guilt by returning to pick up the dry cleaning. But facing the shameful fact that you were being vindictive and mean might be more difficult.

It sounds like a paradox, but we might say that the awfulness of shame is intended to ensure that we do things to make ourselves proud, the point being that we often choose to do things "right" solely because we want to avoid how it feels to slink off with our tail between our legs. Think about it. When you do things you're ashamed of, you generally feel badly about yourself, and when you do things you're proud of, you feel good. Because of its toxicity, shame surely is a powerhouse of a motivator.

✓ STOP AND FEEL

What are you feeling right now?

____

____

____

☼ PRACTICE EXERCISE

Shame vs. Guilt

PURPOSE: To distinguish shame from guilt

RATIONALE: To get the most from your emotions, it's essential to be able to recognize when you are feeling shame and when you are feeling guilt.

WHAT YOU NEED: pen

DIRECTIONS: In the appropriate columns that follow, list the things you feel ashamed of or guilty about. For instance, you might feel ashamed that you didn't go to college, but not guilty. Or you might feel guilty that you missed your grandson's birthday, but not ashamed. Keep adding to the list until you can distinguish guilt from shame.

Shame	Guilt
______________________	______________________
______________________	______________________
______________________	______________________
______________________	______________________

REFLECTION (to be done after completion of exercise): Could you distinguish shame and guilt easily? Which is the more troubling emotion? What could you do to make it less difficult and more bearable?

____

____

____

Can people make me feel ashamed?

As with guilt or any emotion, no one can *make* you ashamed. Of course, this doesn't mean that people won't try to discredit or humiliate you the same way they try to guilt-trip you. Think of yourself as Teflon-coated: no one can make anything stick to you unless you allow it. Assuming that you're honest with yourself (a crucial assumption—are you?), as a mature individual with full cognitive capacities, you can judge your behavior and don't need to take anyone else's judgments as truth.

When deciding if you're feeling shame, it's important to examine the context of the situation. For example, something said may elicit shame in one circumstance but not in another. Let's say you're out to dinner with your best friend who knows you have to take off your shoes and socks to do any kind of arithmetic. When the waiter drops the bill in front of you, she might joke, "Okay, Einstein, hand it over," as she grabs for the check. Now let's imagine that you're at a meeting with your boss and a brand new client when your boss hands you your client's quarterly financial statement and asks you a question about revenues. You're so nervous for a moment that you can't speak and start to stutter, so she quips, "Okay, Einstein, hand it over," as she swipes the statement out of your hand. Same message, different context.

No one can evaluate you like you, as long as you can be honest with yourself. If you're an emotionally healthy person, you should be able to scrutinize yourself and recognize that you have strengths and weaknesses. You know that you're not perfect and never will be and that neither is anyone else. You recognize that you're a worthy individual no matter how much or how little you accomplish in life or how many mistakes you make. When you do something that lives up to your expectations, you feel proud; when you fail to live up to your expectations, you feel shame. If you're going to feel shame, make sure it's the real deal and that you're not buying into it just because someone wants to shame you.

Where does shame come from?

Healthy shame comes from healthy families. Well-balanced parents recognize both their strengths and weaknesses and view their children's behavior with reasonable objectivity. Healthy spouses work on taking responsibility for their mistakes and don't habitually play the blame game. They model healthy shame by being accountable for their behavior and teaching their children to do the same, neither protecting them from feeling appropriately bad nor making excuses when they're at fault. If you grew up in this type of family, consider yourself lucky.

> *In a functional family, shame stings a little to encourage you to become a better person, but the feeling is neither overwhelming nor unbearable.*

You're brought up to learn from mistakes, then let them go. No one is stuck in shame-mode all the time or in a pattern of shame-based behaviors, such as addictions or abuse. Shame does its job—*to get you to look honestly at yourself and mend your ways*—then takes a hike.

However, what do you do if, as a child, your parents and other relatives regularly humiliate you for your shortcomings, make fun of your mistakes, or put you down for your failures? The normal reaction to this kind of ongoing humiliation and debasement is to believe that there is something drastically wrong with you. From that sense of unfixable defectiveness is born a bad case of lifelong shame.

When you're regularly degraded, teased, or demeaned as a child (or as an adult, for that matter), you might lump your wounding into one feeling—"bad." The word functions on two levels: as a mood descriptor and an assessor of self-worth. Whether the underlying belief causes you to feel rotten, or whether feeling rotten grinds you into believing that you're worth nothing, bad is the word that aptly describes exactly how you feel when you're engulfed in shame. And so you wrongly assume, "Because I *feel* bad, I must *be* bad."

Even if you were a basically decent kid and tried hard to please your parents, if they frequently degraded and devalued you, especially if they implied you were never good enough, you're likely to grow up feeling a deep-seated sense of inadequacy and failure. Likewise, if your parents were chock-full of shame and couldn't tolerate their own insecurities, they very likely projected their shame onto you. This means they infused you with it instead of feeling it themselves (also known as the "It-can't-possibly-be-me-so-it's-gotta-be-you" mentality).

However, not all children in a family bear the brunt of shame equally. I've known families where there was equal-opportunity-abuse, in which every child received their share of verbal put-downs and a constant barrage unwarranted blame. I've also come across families where one child was unconsciously singled out to be what's called the *symptom-bearer*. For complex reasons that don't necessarily have anything to do with reality, this particular child gets identified early on as the family scapegoat and suffers the most. The scapegoat or symptom-bearer is the one on whom everyone else projects or dumps their worst fears and feelings about themselves—which, you guessed it—mostly consist of shame. That way only one person in the family is left metaphorically holding the garbage and everyone else can feel squeaky clean.

Being the scapegoat in a shame-based family is one of the worst things that can happen to a child. If you were one, you had to manage everyone else's shame on top of your own. Having no idea that you were the household "dirt bag," you internalized every cruel comment as if it were truth. And then, one of two things happened: Either you believed you were worthless, gave up and became an underachiever or life dropout, or you took your parents' condemnation as a challenge and have spent your whole life defiantly trying to prove them wrong through overachievement and perfectionism. Both reactions are unhealthy and based on your inability to shake off unjustified and undeserved childhood shame.

In another kind of unhealthy family, parents are afraid to allow their children to feel shame and bend over backwards to protect them from it. Though it's understandable that parents would try to minimize their children's emotional pain, this kind of sheltering nearly always backfires because overprotected children end up believing that shame is too unbearable to tolerate. In fact, no matter how hard parents try to shield them, children often feel ashamed anyway. More often than not, they wind up feeling doubly ashamed—for whatever they did and because they think they're not capable of tolerating warranted blame.

When we don't know how to bear shame, we can't take responsibility for ourselves, fix our broken parts, fit into society, or bounce back from failure. If your parents did everything in their power to prevent you from feeling this emotion—took the blame for your misdeeds, minimized your failures, ignored your mistakes, faulted other people for your wrong-doings—they did you a grave disservice because you have to learn how to tolerate and deal with shame in order to be a healthy, well-balanced individual—and to end dysfunctional eating.

✓ STOP AND FEEL

What feelings are getting stirred up as you think about how your family handled blame and shame?

____

____

____

☼ PRACTICE EXERCISE

Pin the Tail on the Donkey

PURPOSE: To understand how shame got assigned and displaced in your family of origin

RATIONALE: To only carry our own shame and not someone else's, we need to understand how shame got played out in the dynamics of our family of origin

WHAT YOU NEED: Two different-color crayons, pen

FORMAT: Need a page or half-page with about six stick figures with lines under them for names.

DIRECTIONS: Think about the dynamics in your family of origin. Was there a scapegoat, a donkey that everyone tried to pin something on? Was that person you? A brother or sister? Or one of your parents? On the line under each stick figure below write the name of each member of your family, including anyone who lived with you. Under that, pick one color crayon and write what they got blamed for that they *should* have (say, your brother truly was never on time or your dad really was a terrible driver). Under that, using a different color, write what they got blamed for that they *shouldn't* have (say, your sister was smart but was told she was stupid or your disabled grandmother got blamed for using up the family's money).

REFLECTION (to be done after completion of exercise): This can be a painful exercise because it entails getting in touch with the shame that existed in your family of origin. Could you identify a scapegoat in your family? Can you distinguish between who *deserved* blame and who *received* it? If you're uncomfortable thinking about these issues, take a few deep breaths until you're feeling better, then return to the exercise.

____

____

____

BELIEFS ABOUT SHAME

Because rational thinking leads to rational behavior, it's essential that you build a belief-system that's sound and healthy. Here are examples of irrational thoughts turned into rational ones.

IB: People can make me feel ashamed.
RB: No one can make me feel ashamed.
Only I can make myself feel ashamed.

IB: I can't bear feeling ashamed.
RB: I can bear feeling ashamed and any other feeling I have.

IB: Shame means I must have done something terrible.
RB: Shame means I feel badly about something I've done.

IB: I should be ashamed of my overeating or undereating.
RB: I feel proud that I'm working on improving my relationship with food.
Undereating or overeating are not shameful behaviors.

IB: I should be ashamed of my weight and my body.
RB: No matter what size I am, I feel good about my body.
I can work on changing my weight without being ashamed of it.

Now it's your turn to transform your irrational beliefs into sound, functional ones. Take your time and make sure each new, rational belief feels right for you. They should be concrete and written in the present tense using an active verb. Feel free to use the list above, but make sure you come up with some of your own as well.

Irrational Belief	**Rational Belief**
____________________	____________________
____________________	____________________
____________________	____________________
____________________	____________________

What does shame-based behavior mean?

Shame-based behavior is that which chronically leaves you feeling ashamed or which *should* leave you feeling ashamed. Getting tipsy one night and flirting with your husband's boss at a retirement party may give you a pinprick of shame when you sober up. Getting drunk and openly flirting with every man except your husband at every social occasion is shame-based behavior. Blowing up at your roommate for not tidying up his mess may make you cringe when you think about it the next day. Blaming your roommate for every problem in your life is shame-based behavior.

In another kind of shame-based behavior, strange as it sounds, you live your life in such a way that you chronically or frequently end up with shameful feelings. That is, you make poor choices (unconsciously) because you truly believe that you don't deserve to feel proud of yourself and because the feeling is familiar from childhood. If you're engaged in this kind of recurring behavior, you most likely had a childhood that was filled with pervasive negativity and are so used to feeling shame that it's uncomfortable to feel good about or proud of yourself. Shame-based behavior includes a pattern of any of the following: anti-social acts which may or may not lead you to court or jail; excessive drinking, drugging, gambling, working, shopping, eating, or exercising; being verbally, emotionally, physically, or sexually abusive; taking unnecessary risks, including acting out sexually, physically, or financially; secretly doing things you know are not in your best interest; and regularly depriving yourself of things you love.

You know a behavior is shame-based because deep down inside, no matter how much you try to deny it or convince yourself otherwise, you don't feel proud. Shame-based behavior has you constantly trying to convince or assure yourself (or others) that what you're doing is just fine. It's often couched in terms of, "I know I shouldn't, but…" Doing something you know is wrong is a sure-fire way to stoke the shame flame.

Shame-based behavior happens when you:

- are doing well but chronically sabotage your success
- ignore the advice of healthy people whom you trust and engage in a relationship or activity that has a high risk of hurting you
- consistently take risky or self-harming actions and try to hide or deny them

- regularly neglect your health and don't take good care of body, mind and spirit
- habitually act on impulse with slight or no regard for consequences

If you want to reduce shame, you will need to start thinking about the consequences of your actions. If you determine that behaving in a certain way will make you feel good about yourself, then that's what you need to do; if the behavior will bring you shame, then it's definitely the wrong choice. If you want to feel proud, you have to build your self-worth, not tear it down. One of the best ways to develop high self-esteem and sound self-worth is to make conscious, intentional choices that you know are in your long-term best interest.

✓ *STOP AND FEEL*

Are you feeling ashamed of any behaviors right now?

____

____

____

How does feeling shame drive me to focus on food and weight?

Because shame may feel unbearable at times, it's a highly challenging emotion, truly one of the most abrasive to our sensitive souls. If you're not used to sitting with such intense discomfort, you may use a food or weight obsession to minimize or avoid the shame of something that happened recently or long ago. The irony is that if you eat when you're not hungry, don't eat when you are, eat past fullness or satisfaction, or don't regularly feed yourself with nourishment and pleasure in mind, you and I both know exactly how you're going to end up feeling—ashamed! So, it's important to recognize that disordered eating serves a dual purpose: It both alleviates *and* perpetuates shame. Moreover, you inadvertently double your dose of discomfort by using food inappropriately to avoid whatever shame you felt initially.

If you're prone to shame-based behavior, using food in an unhealthy way may be your least shameful pattern. Alternately, your food abuse may be your only shame-based activity, the place where you dump all your bad feelings about who you think you are. Or, you may expect so much of yourself in most areas of your life that eating is the only one in which you let yourself go. What all your behaviors have in common, though, is that they destroy feelings of self-love and self-worth.

Rigid or highly-controlled eating on a regular basis also stems from shame, or more precisely, an intense fear of it. Restrictive eaters keep themselves on a short leash around food because they're scared that once they get started, they'll never stop (which, of course, would generate enormous shame for them). Remember when I said that growing up in a family in which parents projected their shame onto their children may produce individuals who are over-achievers and perfectionists.

If you're one of these people, you may micromanage your diet to prove to yourself that you're tough, in control of excess, in charge of your life, and self-disciplined.

The sad truth is that you really *don't* trust your ability to regulate yourself, and so you put all your energies into artificial, excessive control. Desperate to believe you have the right stuff, you try to distance yourself from any (normal) imperfection. Denial of nourishment and sensory delight is your way of reassuring yourself that you've conquered what seems like a shameful desire for food. Sadly, you replace shame not with real pride, but with false pride.

The likelihood is that your perfectionism is motivated by the irrational belief that, "If I'm perfect, I'll never have to feel shame." Unfortunately, perfectionism feeds on itself—the more you fear the shame of imperfection (that is, vulnerability, emotion, excess, etc.), the more perfect you have to be. If you tend toward being a perfectionist, it's important to have areas in your life in which you give yourself permission to make a mess because, well, life is messy! By giving yourself the go-ahead to indulge, you eliminate the assumption that you're doing something wrong. You could also refuse to feel badly about yourself even when you overeat or withdraw from food and decide, instead, to love yourself no matter what. You could do as I do and have at least one or two big, messy piles in an otherwise neat house that remind me that I'm human and perfectly imperfect! When they get so big that they're about to topple over, I go on a filing frenzy, then promptly start a new mess the next day.

Secretive eating or concealing destructive eating behaviors is always shame-based. Shame thrives on secrecy, which means keeping information hidden from ourselves and others. Think about it—the rest of the family is watching TV in the family room and you're locked in the bathroom downing a pint of mocha chip ice cream, terrified of being found out. Or you tell your family you have work to do during dinner and take your food to your room or study, knowing full well that behind closed doors, it'll all go in the trash.

Perfectionism feeds on itself—the more you fear the shame of imperfection, the more perfect you have to be.

Can you see how you double your shame by eating in the bathroom or tossing out your food in private? You may feel as if you're protecting yourself from prying eyes, but what you're doing is reinforcing unhealthy behavior. You'd actually be better off if you felt guilt rather than shame over either behavior because guilt says that you don't like what you're doing and can correct it, while shame says that nothing can make up for the awful person you believe yourself to be.

The goal is to work toward moving all of your eating out into the open, which announces, *"I may not be doing something that's healthy for me, but I'm not going to hide as if I'm a criminal. I'm going to try to understand this behavior and recognize it as shame-based."* When you use food in ways that make you unhappy, you can always make the choice to view your behavior neutrally. You may still wish you had acted differently, but you don't have to worsen your situation by self-shaming. Reacting neutrally to your actions may not take away all of your shame, but it will certainly increase your pride.

Shame is a very, very tough emotion to experience and handle. The best way to detoxify it is through compassion for self, acceptance of all of your behaviors, believing that you're doing the best you can, remaining curious about your motivation, and trying to do better next time. If you can understand your behavior, as opposed to vilifying yourself for it, you have a good shot at changing it. And, when your actions around food become healthier, you'll feel less shame. You may still have to learn to tolerate this bear of an emotion, but at least you won't be using food to make yourself feel worse.

FURTHER EXPLORATION

1. How do you know when you're feeling ashamed?

____

____

____

2. What is the difference between shame and embarrassment?

____

____

____

3. What is the difference between guilt and shame?

____

____

____

4. What is the purpose of healthy shame?

____

____

____

5. Why can't people make you feel ashamed?

____

____

____

6. How does your perfectionism feed into shame?

7. How does your experience with shame as a child affect your ability to tolerate or bear shame today?

8. How did each of your parents manage shame?

9. How would you describe *shame-based* behaviors and which ones do you engage in?

10. How did your parents' shame-based behaviors influence you?

11. How does eating or rigidly controlling your food intake contribute to your shame?

12. What are three effective things you can do to detoxify your shame?

7

Helplessness

(Who Put My Brain in a Straightjacket?)

Helplessness is one of the most challenging feelings we encounter for a few reasons. First and foremost is the intense physical and emotional discomfort it provokes. Moreover, we may fear that if we don't keep helplessness at bay, it will lead to other seemingly-unbearable affects such as hopelessness and despair.

Another reason that we try at all cost to avoid feeling helpless is that our lack of control is like a small death, a nasty reminder of our insignificance in the larger scheme of things and a big chunk of existential angst to swallow. On some level, we all want to believe that we're immortal, and accepting the fact that from dust we come and to dust we shall return can be difficult. Paradoxically, we both know and fight this truth.

The primary difficulty we have with helplessness, however, is that it often arises along with other challenging emotions and may be confused with, overshadowed, or masked by them. Although these emotions may also remain unacknowledged or unidentified, feeling helpless is far more easily missed or misinterpreted.

Why don't I recognize helplessness?

Helplessness goes unrecognized, in part, because other affects are more familiar and dominant: *disappointment* over not getting the promotion you were promised, *anxiety* that you'll miss your plane, *panic* after you've left your purse in the cab, *shock* that your apartment has been burglarized, *grief* when someone you love has died, *fear* that you're being stalked, or *anger* when your teenager takes the car without permission. In each instance, notice how your helplessness takes a back seat to more recognizable and tolerable feelings, rescuing you from deeper, unfamiliar pain.

Take a minute to imagine two cartoons—one of someone feeling anger or high anxiety, what I call "rescue emotions," and another of someone feeling helplessness. The angry person might have a beet red face and be large or oversized, about to burst. The anxious one might radiate kinetic energy and be running around in circles. But the helpless person would be tiny or shrunken, perhaps cowering, and even colorless. Anger gives us a charge, priming us to take on the world; anxiety generates a dynamic sense of activity. Both cover and disguise our impotence. No wonder we welcome them as rescuers!

Although perfectly natural, when you fail to recognize and acknowledge helplessness, and instead, experience and express anger or anxiety, you're not doing what's best for yourself in the long run. Anger—also felt as irritation or impatience—often puts people off, while anxiety takes its toll on body and mind. Moreover, by leap-frogging over helplessness, you lose a valuable opportunity to experience the entire spectrum of emotions and to effectively deal with whatever problem is at hand.

For example, let's say that on the day you're about to move into a new apartment, your landlord calls to say that her current tenants refuse to leave and that it may take weeks to get them evicted. Your mouth drops open as you flash on your boxed-up belongings and the U-Haul at the curb. In a rage, you may chew out your landlord and threaten to call a lawyer. Or, anxious that you'll end up homeless, you may start babbling a mile a minute. Note that both anger and anxiety are a *reaction* to your initial experience of helplessness.

Remember that your emotions are there to get your needs met. Anger simply will not do the job because its intensity and tunnel vision cloud clear thinking; anxiety or stress inflate the situation, often turning a minor problem into a major catastrophe. In both cases, your so-called rescuers actually get in the way of successful problem solving. As long as you keep helplessness hidden under your mental rug, more familiar and tolerable emotions will keep popping out and leading you astray.

Although you may dread that connecting to your helplessness will cause despair, you must bear the feeling to learn what it has to teach you. Tolerating the very stuckness or paralysis you're fighting against is the *only* way to achieve clarity and effectively address your problem. I know it's a great deal to ask that you not give in to more tolerable feelings, but you'll have to deal with your powerlessness and impotence sooner or later—so why not when they first occur? If you're someone who generally leads with anger or who panics at the slightest twist in the road, you'll have to pay special attention to see if these feelings are authentic, or if they're camouflaging helplessness. My bet is that nine times out of ten, it's the latter.

✓ STOP AND FEEL

How are you feeling about learning to sit with helplessness and not converting it to anger or anxiety?

____

____

____

How do I know if I'm feeling helpless?

Many people go through life battling helplessness at every turn without ever knowing it. The experience causes you to feel trapped, stuck, paralyzed, like a deer caught in headlights; you feel vulnerable, useless, irrelevant, insignificant, and occasionally invisible. When the emotional tension gets to be too much, it can easily turn into anger, anxiety, or even despair. However, when you stop fighting it, helplessness will eventually lead you to a better place: surrender and acceptance or solutions that will empower you. Either way, ride out the feeling and you'll eventually be able to move on.

☼ *PRACTICE EXERCISE*

Connecting to Helplessness

PURPOSE: To help you connect to feeling helpless

RATIONALE: By practicing experiencing helplessness, you'll learn a lot about the emotion, especially how to identify it by physical sensations.

WHAT YOU NEED: a room with furniture in it, a good imagination

DIRECTIONS: Look around the room and find something you positively cannot do, such as touch the ceiling without jumping or using anything to stand on, or open a locked door by pulling at it. Pretend that you're in a life-and-death situation and must complete this action. Once you've found this undertaking you know you can't do, try to prove yourself wrong (without hurting yourself, please). If you're trying to touch the ceiling, keeping your feet on the floor, stretch as tall as you can. If your goal is to get that locked door open, pull on it with all your might with one hand, then try it with two. Try to forget that this is an exercise and work on connecting to what helplessness feels like, especially how it feels in your body.

REFLECTION (to be done after completion of exercise): Were you able to pretend hard enough to get in touch with feeling powerless? What sensations did you notice in your body as you tried your impossible task? What was the hardest part of the exercise?

____

____

____

What is the purpose of helplessness?

Helplessness lets you know that a situation is not in your control and there's little or nothing you can do about it, in that exact moment (think of it as energy conservation!). Of course, the helplessness you feel when someone you love dies is different from when you arrive late to pick up your car at the garage and find a "closed" sign on the door. In the first instance, there's nothing to do but acknowledge that you lack the power to bring back your loved one. In the second example, although you may initially feel helpless, there may be actions to take—knock on the door or peek in the windows to see if anyone's still around, call the garage on your cell phone, or have a friend come get you. However, just because you make every attempt to empower yourself doesn't mean you'll find a solution. In the end, you may still be helpless and powerless—and temporarily car-less!

In addition to being completely inevitable and unavoidable, helplessness teaches us modesty and humility by reminding us that we're mere mortals and not gods. It puts us in our place by making us feel tiny and insignificant, as if we're of no consequence at all, and challenges our childish (but understandable) wish to be the center of the universe. It's just not possible to always have our way or our say or be in control. Perhaps helplessness is a way of preparing us for our most inevitable loss of control—death.

BELIEFS ABOUT HELPLESSNESS

Because rational thinking leads to rational behavior, it's essential that you build a belief-system that's sound and healthy. Here are examples of irrational thoughts turned into rational ones.

IB: I should always be in control of my life.
RB: It's natural not to be in control of life sometimes.

IB: I can't tolerate feeling helpless.
RB: I can bear feeling helpless and any other feeling I have.
RB: Bearing helplessness is hard, but doable.

IB: Feeling helpless means I'm incompetent and inadequate.
RB: Feeling helpless does not necessarily come from incompetence or inadequacy.

IB: If I could control my life, I'd be happier and wouldn't have an eating problem.
RB: I can be happier with my life and improve my eating without having more control.

IB: I can't help overeating or undereating.
RB: I can practice eating "normally" and overcome my food problems.

IB: Other people need to change so I won't feel so helpless.
RB: I can't change other people, but I can change myself and feel less helpless.

Now it's your turn to transform your irrational beliefs into sound, functional ones. Take your time and make sure each new, rational belief feels right for you. They should be concrete and written in the present tense using an active verb. Feel free to use the list above, but make sure you come up with some of your own as well.

Irrational Belief	**Rational Belief**
______________________	______________________
______________________	______________________
______________________	______________________
______________________	______________________

Why is helplessness so unbearable?

You have only to think of the time in your life when you had no real power to answer to this question. As an infant, unable to recognize and label emotions, you nevertheless felt every sensation to the depth of your highly impressionable tiny being. And, in those first few months and years, the sensation you felt most frequently was helplessness. In adulthood, you might think that your infant self was disappointed when it wanted to be picked up and no one came, even resentful when its food source was nowhere to be found. But remember, in order to label emotions, you have to be conscious of them, and your baby self lacked the brain structures to perform higher order thinking. You were aware of overwhelming, primitive affect and nothing more—pleasure or pain, comfort or discomfort, gratification or frustration.

So one critical reason that helplessness feels unbearable is that it involves exceedingly intense negative sensations, stored away in your memory bank, from a time when you could not understand or control your emotions. The memory of this potent, overpowering affect may get triggered every time you're in circumstances in which you lack control, even when it's over minor irritants like forgetting where you put your car keys or running out of detergent. Moreover, as a vulnerable infant, you were flooded with other sensations along with helplessness—terror, panic, alarm, powerlessness, and being overwhelmed (not to mention the physical discomfort of being wet and hungry). With repetition, these feelings got encoded together in your brain, so that now it's practically impossible to feel helplessness by itself, that is, without fearing loss of control and associating it with something bad happening.

Two other natural companions to feeling helpless are hopelessness and despair. If you feel scared and powerless long enough, you'll eventually doubt that things will ever get better and you may want to give up. How much hopelessness and despair you experience depends, in part, on the situation and on how long and how often you were helpless while growing up. If you were attended to and given comfort and gratification in a timely manner, you learned that the feeling does end, and that things generally turn out all right if you can just wait it out. On the other hand, if you were neglected or couldn't depend on the people in your life, you may fall into hopelessness and despair fairly quickly now when things don't go your way. In fact, it's often not the impotence or stuckness that's so unbearable, but the dread that it will never end.

I hope you now understand that helplessness feels intolerable because it catapults you back to your weakest, most vulnerable moments. No wonder anger and anxiety seem like the perfect antidotes to paralysis. But remember, the better you are experiencing being helpless and letting it move you toward acceptance or problem solving, the less often you'll need to call upon rescue emotions (or a focus on food) to alleviate your pain.

✓ STOP AND FEEL

What are you feeling right now?

____

____

____

☼ PRACTICE EXERCISE

Help for Helplessness

PURPOSE: To learn to regulate feelings by changing self-talk

RATIONALE: What you tell yourself has a direct bearing on how you feel and act. Change the message, and you will act and react differently.

WHAT YOU NEED: memories

DIRECTIONS: Think of a recent instance or one from the past in which you felt extremely helpless. Paint a vivid scene in your mind and pretend you're back there right now. Intensify your affect by what you tell yourself (for example, it's too scary; I can't bear it; this is going to turn out awful; life isn't fair). Notice how what you say escalates your suffering. Now de-escalate by saying soothing things (for example, I'll get through this; I can bear it; this too shall pass; I'm going to be all right) and giving yourself physical comfort (hugs really help when you're feeling helpless!).

Soothing self-talk:

____

____

____

REFLECTION (to be done after completion of exercise): Does your self-talk generally soothe or exacerbate your helplessness? When you pay attention to negative self-talk, are you able to change it? How might you minimize escalating chatter and maximize self-calming?

____

____

____

Can I avoid feeling helpless?

Neither you nor anyone can avoid feeling helpless occasionally because life is unpredictable and much of it is not in your control. Natural disasters will occur randomly and unexpectedly, people you love will die, you'll grow sick and old, those who hold power over you will exercise it, accidents will happen, and fate will knock the best laid plans off course. Everyone experiences moments or periods of helplessness—the heavy-duty price we pay for renting space on the planet.

> *Although you can't always avoid helplessness, you don't need to court it.*

You can be thoughtful and far-sighted, consider the short- and long-term consequences of your actions, and plan your life accordingly. Flexibility also helps. If you're driving a pre-mapped route and come across a barrier in the road that says "danger," finding a detour rather than driving straight ahead makes sense. Similarly, a healthy combination of sound planning, common sense, *and* flexibility will go a long way toward eliminating a good deal of helplessness. But it can never eradicate it all.

Buddhist philosophy speaks directly to this point in teaching that there are two types of suffering: voluntary and involuntary. *Involuntary suffering* is universal, what every human being must endure, and includes some of the threats to emotional and physical security that I mentioned earlier, such as natural disasters, accidents, illness, and death. *Voluntary suffering*, however, comes from attachment to outcomes, i.e., *wanting*. Now, of course, there are all sorts of wanting, and everybody wants different things: season tickets for the Knicks, for your child to be happy, a meaningful career, to live long enough to see your grandson graduate from law school, for Brad Pitt or Nicole Kidman to fall in love with you, or a slice of key lime pie. Big differences.

The nature of wanting is a partial predictor of the degree of potential suffering and your consequent feelings of helplessness. If what you want is rational and realistic, you *may* be able to avoid the pain of not getting it. If, however, what you want is irrational and completely pie in the sky, you might be setting yourself up for big-time disappointment. Being thoughtful and a good planner helps. Just remember that there are no guarantees, and as the bumper sticker says, *Shit happens!*

The best you can do is:

1) accept that if you're going to remain alive, you're bound to experience occasional feelings of helplessness,
2) learn how to recognize this challenging emotion, and
3) become skilled at bearing it. A wonderful adage is to hope for the best and expect the worst.

Spending your life trying to avoid feeling helpless is like spitting into the wind or trying to hold back the tides. What is natural and inevitable will always win out.

One particular kind of helplessness that you actually *can* avoid, however, is called *learned helplessness*. The term means exactly what it says, that in your childhood you were taught to act *as if* you were helpless when you really were not. This may have happened when you tried to take charge of your life and your autonomy was curtailed because it threatened your parents. To please them or avoid rejection or punishment, you may have had to act incompetent, inadequate, dumb, or dependent. If this was the case, you probably did what children generally do to gain approval and avoid punishment—you adapted to your parents' wishes. Today you may act helpless even when you're not in order to get attention or approval or to avoid punishment and withdrawal of love. Think about it: Do you succumb to learned helplessness?

PRACTICE EXERCISE

What to Do With Helplessness

PURPOSE: To recognize when you are truly helpless and when you're not

RATIONALE: It's essential to understand the difference between needing to accept a situation or finding solutions to change it.

WHAT YOU NEED: pen

DIRECTIONS: Write your responses under the columns below. In the first column, list the things that cause you to feel helpless and truly are unchangeable and unfixable. In the middle column, jot down situations or circumstances that you may think of as unalterable, but which you really can do something about. In the last column, write your action responses to fix the problem. The goal is to reduce column two and expand column three.

REAL HELPLESSNESS	PERCEIVED HELPLESSNESS	SOLUTIONS
____________	____________	____________
____________	____________	____________
____________	____________	____________
____________	____________	____________

REFLECTION (to be done after completion of exercise): Were you surprised that there are things you can do to alleviate feeling helpless? Were you equally surprised that there are things that you just plain have to accept? What was it like to try and distinguish the two? Did coming up with solutions make you feel more empowered?

____

____

____

How does feeling helpless drive me to focus on food and weight?

Zeroing in on food when life zigs instead of zags is more than a distraction to drive away powerlessness. For mere diversion, you could go to a movie or take a walk, call a friend or read a book. In food, you are seeking not only a change of focus and a lessening of pain, but also a way to defy helplessness.

There are so very many ways that we are at the mercy of the fickle finger of fate that it sometimes seems that what we're in charge of equals a big, fat zero. Your friend cancels out on a ski trip at the last minute and you're left with nothing to do all weekend. Your son gets into a fight at school and you need to leave work for the principal's office when you'd planned to spend the afternoon catching up on paperwork. You return from the doctor's office, having been diagnosed with a cancerous tumor, and there's no one home with whom to share the bad news. In each of these situations, you lack power over a troubling situation and may feel an utter loss of control.

For disordered eaters, this is where the trouble begins: you may feel (and truly believe) that the only thing over which you can exert control is food and your weight, so that is where your energy goes. You can't stop life from running its course without consulting you, but you *can* decide what to put (or not put) into your mouth. Focusing on food gives you the (false) sense of being in the driver's seat whether you're counting calories in your head or whizzing up and down the supermarket aisles assembling a feast for one.

As a restrictive eater, you may react to life's unruliness by exerting control over your body and its appetites. Excessively restricting food intake and pre-occupation with weight is your way of trying to balance or cancel out being buffeted around by waves of change you cannot control. You may not have a say when the world is crumbling around you, but you can *feel* in charge by being hyper-vigilant about the way you eat. Self-discipline, self-restraint, and self-deprivation are all your best attempts to combat lack or loss of power. Unfortunately, they only destroy your health and damage your psyche. Real power comes from sound judgment, being able to go with the flow, and having a receptive ear to your emotions. When you're in over your head, true wisdom comes from knowing whether to float or swim!

> ***Real power comes from sound judgment, being able to go with the flow, and having a receptive ear to your emotions.***

As an overeater or binge-eater, you may find comfort in shopping, cooking, feeding, and cleaning up. Keeping busy through eating provides a misleading sense that all is well. But generally, a driven anger and resentment underlie out-of-control eating, as if the very acts of cutting and slicing and chewing and swallowing can prove who's boss. Alternately, giving in to unfettered eating also may be a way of acting out powerlessness. You're saying, *It doesn't matter what I do, so I'm going to give up and eat whatever I want even if it makes me sick.* Notice the all-or-nothing thinking that insists you're in control of everything—or nothing.

We all want to be master of our fate, but deep down most of us know it's not possible. Finding anchors in life can help when you're feeling especially topsy-turvy. Anchors are things such as friends, passions, meaningful work, and being part of a larger community—things which generally remain static and stable, even when you're feeling bounced around like a load of laundry. The more stability you create in your life, the better you'll be at handling the moments and situations when you feel like just so much flotsam and jetsam.

In summary, no one could blame you for fixating on food when you're feeling helpless. But, doing so will only pull you farther and farther away from what you really want: effective problem-solving skills, a healthy body, respect for your appetites, and to reach your life's goals.

FURTHER EXPLORATION

1. What body sensations do you have when you're feeling helpless?

2. What feelings do you use to cover your helplessness or rescue you from it (anger, anxiety, stress)?

3. What is the hardest part of feeling helpless?

4. How large a part do hopelessness and despair play in your avoidance of helplessness?

5. What do you believe is the purpose of helplessness?

6. How did your parents handle helplessness and how did that affect you?

7. If you suffered a great deal of involuntary helplessness as a child, how might this experience affect your ability to tolerate helplessness today?

____

____

____

8. Do you suffer from learned helplessness? If so, give some examples.

____

____

____

9. What are your secondary feelings about experiencing helplessness?

____

____

____

10. How can you become more aware of helplessness driving you to eat or control your food intake?

____

____

____

11. How could you handle helplessness more effectively?

____

____

____

8

Anxiety

(It Can't Find Me if I'm Hiding Behind the Refrigerator!)

Anxiety is the perfect illustration of what *all* feelings are meant to do: move us toward that which is life-enhancing and away from that which is life-threatening. Anxiety is the neon sign that flashes: *watch out, beware, caution, danger!* It may arise from a thought (imagining yourself on a stage singing in front of 200 people) or from actual experience (stepping on that stage to perform). The intent of anxiety, more obviously than any other emotion, is to keep us safe and out of harm's way.

Worrying is one symptom of anxiety with which we're all familiar. But being anxious also produces more subtle manifestations—stress and muscle tension, ongoing angst about the future or constant mental reworking of the past, flashes of panic or fear, obsessions and compulsions, avoidance of specific situations (especially social occasions), making mountains out of molehills, or a generally negative mentality. It can rear up suddenly on the way to meet your blind date, paralyze you from moving on after a divorce, or nearly stop your heart when the telephone rings in the middle of the night. Anxiety can take on a life of its own and easily overshadow whatever triggered it in the first place.

How do I know if I'm feeling anxious?

The physical symptoms of anxiety are usually more obvious than those of other emotions. When you're anxious, practically every organ in your body is on code red. Your pulse and thoughts race, your heart beats faster, your legs get shaky, your mouth becomes dry, and your chest tightens.

In fact, you may *feel* anxious long before you're able to tack a label on this constellation of physical sensations. You're wound up, your thoughts leap about like Mexican jumping beans, you can't focus on anything for long, or are edgy having people around. Waiting for something to happen while simultaneously dreading it—that's anxiety too.

Many people experience anxiety as irritation, impatience, or anger, which is stoked by underlying feelings of helplessness and a desire for control. Your mind may time-travel into the future, speculating, *What if this? What if that?* in an attempt to make things "right" when you get there. Or you may repeatedly mull over troubling actions or situations from your past in a futile attempt to get them to play out differently.

Other, more chronic signs of anxiety include:

- insomnia
- inability to concentrate
- fatigue and exhaustion when you haven't been particularly physically active
- being accident prone
- breathing difficulties
- recurring headaches
- muscle soreness
- back and neck pain
- digestive problems
- skin rashes that aren't due to allergic reactions

✓ STOP AND FEEL

Can you get in touch with any anxiety about what you're reading, if so, what makes you anxious?

____

____

____

☼ PRACTICE EXERCISE

Body Relaxation

PURPOSE: To practice a relaxation technique

RATIONALE: Learning to physically relax will help clear your mind as well. This is a great exercise because it travels so well.

WHAT YOU NEED: a comfortable position

DIRECTIONS: Starting from your feet and working your way up to the top of your head, tense each muscle group for ten seconds, then relax each one for ten seconds. Then tense and relax again for ten seconds, so that you've done two sets with each muscle group—feet, leg, buttocks, belly, chest, arms and hands, neck and shoulders, head. When you're done, tense your entire body twice for ten seconds and then completely relax.

REFLECTION (to be done after completion of exercise): Did you notice a shift in body tensions? The more you practice this exercise, the more quickly you'll relax. Could you make time in your day to practice it two or three times? How will this exercise help reduce your anxiety?

____

____

____

Is anxiety the same as fear?

We cannot talk about anxiety without discussing fear, which is an automatic, biological reaction that occurs in response to a specific threat or danger—terror of drowning as you raft down the Colorado River or fear about the kidney transplant you're having tomorrow. Fear can be realistic (dread of lung cancer as a life-long smoker) or unrealistic (apprehension about riding in an elevator). The important thing to remember is that fear is a sharply, narrowly-focused response.

Anxiety, on the other hand, is a non-specific and unfocused response to an imagined threat—you're not sure exactly what terrible fate will befall you or someone else, but you believe that *something* bad might happen. Anxiety is usually irrational, involving consequences that may or may not be as grave as you foresee. The fear reaction is innate, while anxiety, to a large extent, is a learned coping response. Think of it this way: you experience fear when a bear charges at you in the woods and anxiety when you contemplate walking alone in the forest when the moon is full.

Because physical responses to fear and anxiety are often strikingly similar, understanding the workings of one will help you better understand the other. As I said earlier, fear is a hard-wired response to danger aimed solely at self-preservation and survival. Our entire race would have died out long ago if primitive humans hadn't had a keenly honed sense of when they were in physical peril. When threats in the environment tripped their danger wire, their instant reaction was to fight, flee, or freeze. There were times, of course, when the fear response worked too well—say, when a person mistook a stick for a snake. But, better that than mistaking a snake for a stick. Too many slip-ups like that and the human race would be extinct!

Is anxiety a good or a bad thing?

Most anxiety is what we call *signal anxiety*, a conditioned response warning of both real and imagined danger. The key, of course, is to discern which threats are valid, logical and likely, and which are scraps of memory, which need no longer trigger alarm.

Signal anxiety works exceedingly well when there's true danger, but becomes counterproductive when the reaction is to a memory or situation that is no longer dangerous. If you go into anaphylactic shock whenever you eat shellfish, you have a darned good reason to become anxious when your dinner hostess serves seafood stew. However, if your heart was broken by a tall, blue-eyed, blond when you were 17 and now you're 34 and have ruled out dating Nordic types on principle, that's anxiety run amuck. If, as a child, your father slapped you every time you answered back and now you can't bring yourself to speak up when someone trashes your feelings, that's misguided anxiety. If you were teased unmercifully by members of the school marching band during practice and now refuse to join any kind of group or organization, that's malfunctioning anxiety.

Your fear made perfect sense when it was doing its job of protecting you from physical or emotional harm as a child, but now that you can take better care of yourself, you don't need anxiety to keep you safe. You have better judgment, more choices, intervening experiences, greater internal resources, and a caring support system.

Is there such a thing as chronic anxiety?

Your fear response system functions similarly to computer anti-virus software, which provides protection from viruses, Trojan horses, worms, and other techno-nasties. In the same way, your innate sensors constantly scan your environment for emotional and physical threats—footsteps quickening behind you on a dark, deserted street, your child running out into traffic, the smell of smoke awakening you in the middle of the night. Your fear response system cues in to these kinds of specific threats to keep you safe and out of harm's way.

Now imagine your anti-virus software alerting you every time it picks up *any* kind of intruder, even an email from your cousin George inviting you to a family picnic. Enough false alarms and you'd never get any work done on your computer: you'd be too busy assessing every so-called threat. In this case, your fear response system is malfunctioning, shifting into high alert repeatedly and unnecessarily. Think of an anxious mind as a system in overdrive, unable to shut down.

Chronic anxiety can make you exert useless energy trying to redo the past. You may ruminate or replay a scenario repeatedly in your mind, not to problem solve, but to assess how it went in order to reassure yourself that all is well. Engaging in rumination sets off a lot of "what ifs" and assumptions that can rarely be verified. Your goal in rummaging through the past is to reduce anxiety, but the activity often has the opposite effect: You become dependent on it, rather than remaining in the present and handling whatever happens.

Anxiety may also mentally project you into the future—what we call worrying—in a futile attempt to foresee and prepare for what will happen down the road. In an attempt to reduce anticipated harm or pain, you may over-plan or create worst-case scenarios in your head. Worrying makes you feel as if you're taking *some* kind of action, even if the activity is only occurring between your ears. When you feel unable to control something that makes you afraid—say, the fact that it's 2 a.m. and you haven't heard from your 18-year-old son who's out with your car—you have to channel that energy *somewhere*. So because there's nothing you can actually do (once you've left a half-dozen messages on his cell phone and awakened all his friends and their folks), you do the one thing you *can* do—worry. Worry is a seeming antidote to anxiety and our old friend helplessness.

Another mental phenomenon that happens when anxiety hijacks common sense is that your thoughts zip around like racecars and you catastrophize. You bounce from imagining your son driving alone on a deserted highway, to the collision you had 12 years ago that totaled your car, to a

TV show you saw last night that involved a truck barreling over a cliff. Before you know it, you're a victim of your thoughts and can't find the "off" switch in your brain.

✓ STOP AND FEEL

What are you feeling right now?

____

____

____

BELIEFS ABOUT ANXIETY

Because rational thinking leads to rational behavior, building a belief-system that's sound and healthy is essential. Here are examples of irrational thoughts turned into rational ones.

IB: People make me feel anxious.
RB: Only I can make myself feel anxious.

IB: I'm just an anxious person and can't change.
RB: I can learn to lessen my anxiety over time.

IB. Focusing on food is the only thing that helps me feel better when I'm anxious.
RB: I can find many ways to feel better when I'm anxious other than focusing on food.

IB: I can't bear feeling anxious.
RB: I can bear feeling anxiety and any other feeling.

IB: If I had more control over my life, I'd never feel anxious.
RB: Feeling anxious occasionally is a normal response to life.

Now it's your turn to transform your irrational beliefs into sound, functional ones. Take your time and make sure each new, rational belief feels right for you. They should be concrete and written in the present tense using an active verb. Feel free to use the list above, but make sure you come up with some of your own as well.

Irrational Belief	**Rational Belief**
____________________	____________________
____________________	____________________
____________________	____________________
____________________	____________________

Are some people more anxious than others?

You bet! Some people are definitely more anxiety-prone, in large part because the emotion has a strong underlying biological component. Researchers now understand and have evidence that suggests how profoundly our biochemistry influences our emotions. In brief, our moods are regulated by brain chemicals called *neurotransmitters*, which, among other things, keep us focused and calm and provide us with a sense of well being.

The five inhibitory neurotransmitters that are most important to regulating anxiety and other key emotions are:

serotonin – soothes and calms us

dopamine – elevates mood

norepinephrine (or *noradrenaline*) – influences how our body reacts to stress and anxiety

glutamine – promotes relaxation

gamma aminobutyric acid (GABA) – helps to relieve nervous tension

Not only do we need a sufficient amount of these chemicals in our brain to regulate our emotions, but they also must occur in the correct balance to keep our moods stable and our emotional system well-oiled.

Imagine how you might feel if you had the perfect balance of neurotransmitters—you'd be generally upbeat, would relax easily, handle stress relatively well, and calm down fairly quickly when you were upset. If something frightened you or made you anxious, except in extraordinary circumstances, you'd be able to soothe yourself and return to your normal state of mind within a short time. Now imagine how you'd feel if you had a neurotransmitter imbalance. You'd have a *much* harder time handling the ups and downs of daily life.

Actually, the situation is a little more complicated because human development always involves both nature and nurture. If your parents had a healthy set of mood-regulators, chances are you will too. Plus, parents who are relatively emotionally stable are likely to raise children who can modulate their moods—barring other causes of emotional disregulation, such as significant trauma.

On the other hand, let's say your parents lacked a healthy complement of these neurotransmitters and passed a similar load down to you. Due to their biochemical imbalance, they may have had trouble managing their own moods and been ineffective at parenting a child with similar tendencies. Hard as they tried, it's all too likely that you grew up to be someone with emotional difficulties comparable to theirs.

> *Both genetics and socialization are at work when it comes to mood regulation.*

It makes sense—for both biological and psychological reasons—that anxious parents often produce anxious children. Factor in the effect of significant stress or trauma, which has a depleting effect on the precise neurotransmitters that modulate anxiety and other emotions, and you may end up with one highly anxious individual.

✓ STOP AND FEEL

If you're feeling at all anxious right now, what might be causing it?

____

____

____

☼ PRACTICE EXERCISE

Comfort Corner

PURPOSE: To self-soothe

RATIONALE: Everyone needs to know how to self-soothe. It's an essential component of emotional self-care.

WHAT YOU NEED: memory

DIRECTIONS: Most of us had a favorite, cozy spot we cherished as children, a "comfort corner" out on the back steps, in the woods, or under the covers. Or perhaps it was in a closet or hidden behind a big pile of pillows. If you had one, your body already associates being there with feelings of safety and security and you can use that memory to relax yourself now. Get comfortable and visualize your comfort corner, calling up every sensory detail you can recall. When you've made the scene come alive, place yourself in it and continue to steep yourself in the sights, smells, sounds, and textures you experienced. Stay in your corner until you feel less anxious, and remind yourself that you can return any time.

REFLECTION (to be done after completion of exercise): Was it easy or hard to conjure up your comfort corner? Did you start to relax as you imagined your old cozy space? Did you give yourself enough time for your body to remember the experience or give up right away when you didn't instantly relax? Remember, visualization is a way to trick your mind into changing its perspective and you can do it anywhere, anytime.

____

____

____

How does feeling anxious drive me to focus on food and weight?

There are a number of ways that anxiety drives a preoccupation with food and weight for both undereaters and overeaters. The first is looking to food and your body, either consciously or unconsciously, to disconnect or distract you from intense affect. More often than not, you may not even realize that heading for the Hagen Daz or for your bathroom scale to recheck your weight may be reactions to feeling keyed up. But just because you're unaware, doesn't mean that anxiety isn't motivating your behavior.

Think about how activities such as rummaging through the refrigerator or running the day's food consumption through your mind in minute detail really do make you forget your troubles—for a while. The mental exercises of calorie counting and comparing how much you ate yesterday to how little you're eating today, as well as the physical behaviors of weighing food and policing your food intake do an excellent job of discharging neurotic energy. So do grocery shopping, poring over cookbooks, food selection and preparation, cooking, eating and cleaning up. The act of eating itself—chomping, chewing and swallowing—also helps releases tension. If you can lose yourself in mind-numbing activities, your heart goes numb as well!

The goal is to act with conscious intent rather than misuse food in an unconscious way.

Re-channeling your energy when you're anxious is not necessarily an unhealthy choice as long as you acknowledge and identify why you're overwound. The goal is to act with conscious intent rather than misuse food in an unconscious way. Once you're aware of what's causing your agitation, you can then move on to find effective, appropriate ways to handle it—call, email, or write to a friend, meditate, do deep breathing, take a walk, go to a movie, watch TV, write in your journal, or pick up a book. Or, if you can, take action that will change your situation so that you don't need to be as anxious. For example, check your tires if you're headed out on a road trip and call ahead to make reservations if you're afraid your favorite restaurant won't have a table for you.

Also, food is a natural when you're anxious because of its soothing biochemical properties. Just as people with alcohol and drug problems self-medicate, so do anxiety-ridden disordered eaters. You may seek out carbohydrates, a food group that produces energy in the short run but also calms you down. Think about how you feel after a Thanksgiving feast of sweet potatoes and gravies, rich desserts, and maybe a couple of glasses of beer or wine. You're so relaxed and drowsy, you could doze off at the table. Isn't that the exact effect you desire when you're seeking to de-stress—foods that will take the edge off and help you unwind?

Another way that food serves anxious, disordered eaters is more subtle. Say, it's 3 a.m. and you *still* haven't heard a word from that son of yours who's out with your car. Your thoughts are spiraling downward while your anxiety is soaring. You can't sleep, so you get up for a little nosh even though you're not the least bit hungry, and end up working your way through the leftovers you planned to serve tomorrow. By the time you're ready to return to bed, you've redirected your anxiety from your son lying dead in a ditch to anger at yourself for all you ate and for feeling stuffed. You've traded in upset about your son for upset over your eating, which is more bearable and familiar.

You may also use your fear of food to quell your unease when you whip out a cookbook and review recipes, start planning your 1,000-calorie-or-less meals for the entire week, decide that now is the perfect time to do a hundred sit-ups, or reassure yourself by going through your closet and trying on your "skinniest" clothes. By the time you're done, you still may not know where your son is, but you feel more in control of yourself and your life. Additionally, there's a soothing quality in numbers—adding up calories or fat grams—that's reminiscent of counting sheep or backwards from one hundred.

Yet another way that anxiety generates an unhealthy preoccupation with food and weight relates to obsessions and compulsions. Obsessive thoughts are irrational, persistent, and repeatedly intrude into consciousness, thereby raising anxiety. Perhaps some of them are familiar to you—*I have to weigh X or I'll never be happy; if there's food in the house, I'll eat it; if I eat I'll get fat; I need to finish all the food on my plate; I must have that Snickers bar right now; I should eat this, I shouldn't have eaten that.*

Compulsions are repetitive behaviors whose sole intent is to reduce anxiety. Some of them may also be familiar to you—weighing yourself repeatedly, cleaning your plate, returning again and again to the mirror to see how thin you are or to make sure you aren't getting fat, finishing off any food you start to eat whether you're full or not, eating when you're not hungry but because the food is there, calculating calories and fat grams for every morsel you put into your mouth, poring over recipes you'll never make, planning out every single thing you're going to eat for the day, or overexercising because you overate.

Are you starting to get the picture? The most effective way you've found to reduce your anxiety about eating and your body is to resort to dysfunctional behavior. You're caught up in a vicious cycle: obsessive thinking leads to compulsive behavior which reinforces obsessive thinking, and so on and so forth. The only way out of this endless loop is to stop your irrational thoughts and/or to tolerate the anxiety generated by them and refrain from compulsive behavior. Not an easy task, but you *can* do it.

Remember, feeling afraid and anxious is a part of life. Fear is natural and necessary, and having occasional anxiety is inevitable. But you don't have to remain a victim. You can make sure that you know when and why anxiety has come to visit, practice relaxing, and use effective ways to re-channel your energy. You can work on reframing irrational beliefs and engaging in sensible self-talk. Lastly, although you can't eradicate anxiety completely, by healing your unhealthy focus on food and weight, you can eliminate one thing that makes you anxious—your dysfunctional eating and destructive relationship with your body!

FURTHER EXPLORATION

1. What are the bodily sensations that indicate you're feeling anxious?

___

___

___

2. What do you think is the purpose of anxiety?

____

____

____

3. If you suffered a great deal of anxiety as a child, how does this experience contribute to your feeling anxious today?

____

____

____

4. Do you experience *signal anxiety*? How does it work for and against you?

____

____

____

5. How did your parents manage anxiety and what did you learn from them about how to handle it?

____

____

____

6. If you have secondary feelings about anxiety, what are they?

____

____

____

7. What situations make you most anxious?

____

____

____

8. How does focusing on food or weight help or hurt you when you're anxious?

____

____

____

9. How does anxiety about eating or gaining weight compare to other anxieties in your life?

____

____

____

10. What are five ways that you could use to handle anxiety effectively?

____

____

____

9

Disappointment

(If I Use My Scale as a Shield, I Won't Feel a Thing!)

Disappointment arises when your needs, wishes, or expectations don't get met. You hope for one thing and end up with another, or with less than you wanted. Disappointments can be large, such as being passed over for a promotion or being left at the altar, or small, as when you can't find those slinky navy sandals in your size. Surprisingly, it's not always major disappointments that knock the wind out of you; seemingly trivial letdowns can feel crushing, too.

You might be disappointed by life in general, by other people, or by yourself (or by all three!). Maybe you hoped to become a ballerina, earn a PhD., live in the mountains, get married, have children, or retire at 40. All of us have dreams throughout our lives and feeling badly when some of them don't come true is normal. But how could it be otherwise when life is a mixed bag of intentional action and pure dumb luck?

One particularly painful kind of disappointment is when you believe you've let yourself down. This experience is familiar to people with eating problems because they often have unreasonable expectations of themselves. Examples include trying to be superwoman (or man) by taking care of everyone, never saying "No" to requests for help, attempting to be or appear perfect, or trying to overcome an eating disorder on your own and refusing to seek help. The truth is, when you ask more of yourself than is realistically possible, you're bound to fail.

How do I know if I'm feeling disappointed?

Getting your hopes up and having them dashed is the ultimate emotional bad landing. When you're disappointed, you experience a sinking feeling, a literal letdown, as if the elevator carrying your heart is hurtling toward the basement, or as if one minute you're coasting along on a spirited breeze of *yes* and suddenly you crash headlong into a concrete wall of *no*. Disappointment not only deflates you, but also reminds you of how high you *could* have flown.

Other strong feelings often accompany disappointment, like sadness, confusion, helplessness, resentment, envy, bitterness, despair, and the shame of being a "loser." When the feeling descends upon you, you may want to cry, punch a wall, sink into sleep, or curl up and die.

✓ STOP AND FEEL

What are your disappointments around food, eating, weight, and your body?

___

___

___

☼ PRACTICE EXERCISE

Identifying Letdowns

PURPOSE: To recognize how you are disappointed by life, other people, and yourself

RATIONALE: It's so easy to slough off disappointment that we often don't recognize how it colors our life. This exercise will help you identify the locus of your disappointment so that you can start to address it.

DIRECTIONS: Have a mini-brainstorming session and fill in the columns below with as many examples as you can think of in each category. When you're done, you may have disappointments spread evenly across all three columns or find that one has significantly more than the other two.

Disappointment List • My letdowns come from:

Life	*Other People*	*Myself*

REFLECTION (to be done after completion of exercise): Were you surprised by what causes most of your disappointment? If it's from the general unfairness of life, what do you have to do to get more of what you want? If it's due to other people, could you make some personnel changes? If you're not living up to your own ideals and aspirations, are you not trying hard enough or are you expecting too much of yourself?

What is the purpose of disappointment?

Although disappointment feels awful, it can provide you with a wealth of valuable information about yourself and your world. Once again, its purpose is to keep you moving toward what's beneficial and away from what's going to come back and bite you. It's meant to teach you how to make realistic, well-informed choices by recognizing the delicate balance between what you have power over and what you don't. Examining disappointment with an open mind will help you distinguish between being foolhardy, childish, or demanding and courageous, generous, and willing to take appropriate risks. In short, it's there to help you get the good things you deserve.

Disappointment will also help you identify who in your life is reliable, dependable, and there for you—and who isn't. It will help you separate what people say—*You know I'd do anything for you*—from what they do, which may fall far short of their promises. Lastly, it shines a spotlight on your desires so that you can determine which of them will lead to fulfillment and which will lead to heartache.

Ironically, some people use disappointment to reinforce how *little* they deserve in life and how they shouldn't get their hopes up. I hear it all the time something fails to work out for a client and they remind me, "See? Nothing good ever happens to me. I've got a black cloud hanging over my head." But, try as I might, I fail to see a cloud, black or otherwise. Instead, I see someone with irrational, self-destructive, negative thinking who's stuck in old wounds, suffered too much disappointment already, and has mistaken their history for their future. Attending to their disappointment could teach them how to heal their hurt, develop a more positive perspective—and move on.

Recognizing and acknowledging what's in your control and what isn't can help shape your expectations and choices. It can put your feelings into perspective when things don't work out as planned and you're licking your wounds. We'd all like to rule the universe, but the wise among us adapt to their own limitations *and* accept the arbitrariness, unfairness, and unpredictability of life.

✓ *STOP AND FEEL*

What do you feel disappointed about right now?

Why does disappointment hurt so badly?

Disappointment packs a wallop whether it catches you by surprise or you're waiting for it to happen. It hurts in order to get your attention. You may even make it worse by convincing yourself that if you're always vigilant and in control, bad things won't happen to you. In this way, you con yourself into believing that things *have to* work out and experience a double whammy when they don't. When you walk around with your hands covering your eyes, you're bound to be shocked if you stumble into a brick wall.

You also deepen disappointment when you insist that everything that doesn't work out is your fault, especially when you use it as affirmation of your worthlessness and a reminder that you're doomed to have unfulfilled dreams and unmet needs. Add to that your self-contempt for feeling like a loser, and you end up sinking lower and lower. Can you see how you compound the hurt with your unhealthy (and untrue) view of yourself? Wouldn't it be better to take appropriate responsibility when things don't work out, rather than adding to your disappointment by beating yourself up?

How did I learn about disappointment?

As with the other strong emotions, the way you experience and react to disappointment has its roots in childhood. If you've been raised by parents who were reliable and predictable, coped fairly well with setbacks, cushioned your letdowns, generally kept their promises, helped put your upset into perspective, and treated you respectfully and fairly, you probably manage pretty well when things don't go your way. You know that disappointment is distressing, but not necessarily overwhelming or intolerable, that you can bear it by marshalling your inner resources and getting support from others, and that it's an inevitable and universal, but only an occasional, condition.

> ***The way you experience and react to disappointment has its roots in childhood.***

However, if your parents coped poorly with disappointment, you had ineffective role models and no one to teach you how to handle setbacks and failures. When things didn't go their way, maybe your dad drank or your mom took to her bed, depressed. Or they yelled and screamed and blamed you or each other. If so, you might have gotten the idea that life should always go smoothly and your way and that anger and blame are appropriate responses when things go wrong. If your folks constantly complained about their circumstances, behaved like perpetual victims, were bitter and resentful, gave up easily or never got their hopes up, you probably acquired a great many negative messages.

If you were blamed frequently for your parents' setbacks and for situations you couldn't control, you may assume that everything bad that happened to you or them was your fault. Believing you had power was your way of trying to minimize your pain. After all, the illusion that you can do better next time and make things come out right is far more tolerable than feeling helpless and despairing. If your parents never took risks in fear of being disappointed, you may think it's so unbearable that you're scared to have aspirations or expectations. You just float along through life taking whatever comes, the good with the bad, pretending you're happy.

If you were faced with overwhelming and/or repeated disappointment while growing up, you have good reason to think that you're a magnet for it. Your experience attests to the fact—or at least that's your perception. Lowering your expectations was a healthy, adaptive mechanism for survival. However—and this is a biggie—that was then and this is now. You're older, wiser, more experienced, and your life circumstances are different. You have more control, more power, and many more choices today.

You may also have difficulty tolerating disappointment if you were overprotected as a child by well-meaning parents who regularly minimized your failures to prevent you from feeling hurt and upset. Maybe they rushed in with excuses and inappropriate, excessive comfort or tried too hard to neutralize your pain, so that you never learned that disappointment is normal and natural. You may have gotten the message that you weren't capable of dealing with intense emotions. No wonder that now, as an adult, you feel incompetent, inadequate, and insecure.

You may not believe that you'll ever be able to reprogram your unhealthy lessons about disappointment, but you will. The first step is to thoroughly examine your beliefs and be honest about how you view not getting what you want. The next step is to decide what healthy, rational beliefs you need and start visualizing yourself acting on them. And the third is to catch yourself when you're in the throes of disappointment and talk yourself into managing it better. Think of it this way—every time you fail to live up to the way you'd like to handle disappointment, you get another chance at bat!

✓ *STOP AND FEEL*

What are you feeling about how your parents modeled and/or taught you to handle disappointment?

____

____

____

☼ *PRACTICE EXERCISE*

Stories of Disappointment

PURPOSE: To identify childhood memories of disappointment

RATIONALE: In order to understand how you view and react to disappointment today, you have to return to the past. It may be painful calling up times when you or your family were let down, but the payoff will be increased understanding of your difficulty with this emotion today.

WHAT YOU NEED: your voice

DIRECTIONS: First, speak aloud a story of a disappointment (major, if possible) that one or both of your parents had to face when you were growing up (for example, losing a job, illness, divorce). Focus on their reaction and how it impacted you. Next, tell a story about a disappointment you suffered, especially if you still feel its sting today (for example, not making a sports team, promises your parents didn't keep). Focus on how you handled the letdown back then and how it still affects you. If you're in the mood, keep telling stories until you run out of disappointments!

REFLECTION (to be done after completion of exercise): Could you make an emotional connection to past situations or are you cut off from the pain of childhood disappointment? Is there a thread that runs through your stories: do you handle disappointment the way your parents did or purposely do the exact opposite when you're heartbroken? Do you see yourself as a victim or generally empowered?

____

____

____

____

____

BELIEFS ABOUT DISAPPOINTMENT

Because rational thinking leads to rational behavior, it's essential that you build a belief-system that's sound and healthy. Here are examples of irrational thoughts turned into rational ones.

IB: I can't bear feeling disappointed.
RB: I can bear feeling disappointed and any other feelings.

IB: If I did things right, I would never be disappointed.
RB: Everyone is disappointed sometimes.

IB: If I chose the right people in my life, I wouldn't be disappointed.
RB: It's natural and expected that people will disappoint me occasionally.

IB: Nothing ever goes right in my life.
RB: I have things in my life that go well and things that don't.

IB: I have a black cloud hanging over my head and will never be happy.
RB: I can make choices that make me happy.
RB: No one is pre-ordained to be happy or unhappy throughout life.

IB: If I weren't so needy, I wouldn't be disappointed so much.
RB: Everyone has legitimate needs.

IB: I have to get what I want right away or I'll be upset.
RB: I can not get what I want and still feel okay.

Now it's your turn to transform your irrational beliefs into sound, functional ones. Take your time and make sure each new, rational belief feels right for you. They should be concrete and written in the present tense using an active verb. Feel free to use the list above, but make sure you come up with some of your own as well.

Irrational Belief	**Rational Belief**
____________________	____________________
____________________	____________________
____________________	____________________
____________________	____________________

If I weren't so needy, would I be disappointed less?

If you're frequently disappointed, you might assume it's because you're asking for more than you deserve or that you have needs (physical, emotional, intellectual, sexual, or spiritual) that are too numerous, inappropriate, oversized, or burdensome. Worse, you may believe that you shouldn't have needs at all. You're right that you'd never be disappointed if you didn't have any, but we all do—whether they're called wants, wishes, expectations, hopes, yearnings, dreams, or desires. In any case, it's *not* necessarily true that having fewer needs would lessen your disappointment; the subject is far more complicated than that.

Here's why. Sometimes, without realizing it, you may act in ways that hinder your needs from being met and lead you to feeling disappointed. For example, say you make plans for a movie with a friend who has a rotten track record of reliability—a bad habit of canceling dates or not showing up at all. There you are outside the theatre waiting for 25 minutes when she hurries over, breathless and brimming with excuses. Of course you're upset because the show has sold out and the movie's already started. In this situation, knowing about your friend's chronic unreliability, you've put yourself in a situation that upped your odds of being disappointed. Setting yourself up in this way is the kind of voluntary suffering discussed in Chapter 7.

Here are other examples of voluntary disappointment: You expect your parents to love and respect you even though they never have, go on the same fad diet over and over and expect to keep the weight off, trust your friend with a secret although he's a blabbermouth, are desperate to squeeze into a size 2 when your tall, strong, athletic body is a perfect size 8, or say "Yes" to a night out drinking with co-workers even though you almost always return home drunk and depressed. What all these scenarios have in common is that you're wearing rose-colored glasses and not looking clearly at your part in producing a negative reality.

You also may unconsciously set yourself up for disappointment and feeling too needy if you have a false sense of *entitlement, unrealistic expectations*, or engage in *magical thinking. Entitlement* comes from behaving as if you deserve more than the next gal or guy and should receive rewards without having to earn them. Signs include frequently demanding special treatment, putting yourself above the rules, insisting that every whim be gratified (and gratified now!), and making requests that are way out of the ordinary. *Unrealistic expectations* are just that—they simply ain't gonna happen—Matt Damon is not going to suddenly appear on your doorstep and you won't be attending Harvard with your D-plus average. *Magical thinking* describes a blatant refusal to see reality because the truth hurts too much and fantasizing feels more comfortable, secure, and hopeful. Magical thinking is in play when you and your fiancé fight all the time, but you anticipate a loving marriage, or when you continue to hang out with friends who support your practice of bulimia, but still think you can stop on your own.

If you believe you're getting more than your share of disappointment and that many of your important wants and wishes frequently go unmet, now is a good time to look squarely at what you are asking of yourself, others, and life. You can start by making sure that your expectations are rational and realistic and that they can be met effectively. If you have questions about their appropriateness, check them out with a close friend (or a professional).

If you tend to feel entitled, you can work on developing patience and humility, which go a long way toward making people want to respond to your valid needs. If you incline toward magical thinking, try to understand your attachment to denial and your fears about facing the cold, hard truth. Changing your thinking is hard, hard work, so you might want to seek out a therapist to help you identify irrational thoughts and develop a rational belief system.

Two things need to happen if you want less disappointment in your life. You have to make sure your desires and expectations are rational, realistic, and appropriate and that you're not sabotaging yourself unconsciously. You also have to surround yourself with people who wholeheartedly want the best for you, which means they're willing to take your needs seriously and make a reasonable attempt to meet them. If you don't have this kind of healthy support, make time to consider why and how to get it. This may mean reducing contact with people who don't have your best interests at heart as well as making new friends who do. A tall order? To be sure. But just think how great it will feel to get what you want and deserve out of life.

✓ STOP AND FEEL

How do you feel about the quality and quantity of your needs?

____

____

____

☼ PRACTICE EXERCISE

Courting Disappointment

PURPOSE: To understand how you set yourself up for disappointment

RATIONALE: You can avoid some letdowns by figuring out what you do unconsciously to invite them and by changing your expectations, actions, and reactions.

DIRECTIONS: Consider times when you've been disappointed during the last week or month. As you come up with examples, list them in the appropriate column based on their cause—Voluntary Disappointments, Feeling Entitled, Unrealistic Expectations, or Magical Thinking. Don't stop until you can easily identify if you have a hand in your disappointment.

VOLUNTARY DISAPPOINTMENT	FEELING ENTITLED	UNREALISTIC EXPECTATIONS	MAGICAL THINKING
____________	____________	____________	____________
____________	____________	____________	____________
____________	____________	____________	____________
____________	____________	____________	____________
____________	____________	____________	____________

REFLECTION (to be done after completion of exercise): Being honest with yourself is hard, isn't it? What did you learn about your disappointments? Do you have more of a hand in them than you thought? Try to understand what's behind your unhealthy patterns of placing yourself in situations or in engaging in behavior that's bound to hurt you.

____

____

____

How does feeling disappointed drive me to focus on food and weight?

If you're like many disordered eaters, you lack faith in your ability to console yourself when you're in the throws of disappointment and/or feel awkward or fearful of burdening other people with your troubles. Instead of turning to friends for comfort or a new perspective, you look to various food behaviors to distract you, pick you up, or set your world right. You prefer to tough it out alone, ashamed that you might have been the cause of things not working out or because you believe that if you'd only tried harder they would have. Or you lift your spirits by getting psyched for another diet or reading over your food journal to reassure yourself how little you ate for the day.

If you're someone who eats when things don't work out, food may actually seem like a good friend—it never turns a cold shoulder, says it's too busy, ignores, laughs, or yells at you. Plus, when you're eating, you feel safe, comforted, fulfilled, and maybe even happy. Food seems a perfect counterweight to the deflation of disappointment. But down the line, usually after the last swallow, you realize your mistake and back comes that sinking feeling in spades. Now you're facing whatever brought you down in the first place *and* unhappiness with yourself for being conned into thinking that food would make you feel better. Or you've replaced an unfamiliar, scary disappointment (whatever bummed you out) with an old familiar one (your lack of control around food).

If you're a restrictive eater, disappointment might send you into such a tailspin that the only way you know to stop spinning is to grab hold of something, and that something usually relates to food and your body. You may not be master of your universe, but you can exert control where you think it really matters by not eating, rigidly restricting your food intake, refusing to go to dinner with friends, or jumping onto the scale to feel proud about how little you weigh. The rest of your life may bring you down, but at least you don't have to disappoint yourself by gaining weight.

The fact is, though, that when you fixate on food to cushion disappointment, you're not really taking away the regret, but adding to it. Now you feel badly for your destructive behavior *and* the fact that you couldn't face your feelings. You've created a vicious cycle, because more acting out with food will only bring more disappointment in yourself.

There are two effective ways to break this cycle. You can sit with your feeling and try to soothe yourself and let it pass, which builds inner resources and makes you stronger emotionally. Or you can turn to someone else for comfort and cheering up, which builds external resources through deeper connections. Although these behaviors can feel risky, they're bound to increase your self-pride. Plus, by learning to depend on yourself and others, you'll be moving toward facing disappointment head on. Then, even though you may struggle with the feeling itself, you'll feel better about how you've handled it.

FURTHER EXPLORATION

1. How do you know when you're disappointed?

___

___

___

2. What is the purpose of disappointment?

___

___

___

3. If you suffered a great deal of involuntary disappointment as a child, how does this experience contribute to your difficulties today?

___

___

___

4. What is the worst thing about feeling disappointed?

______

______

______

5. How did your parents handle their own disappointment and what did you learn from them about this feeling?

______

______

______

6. How did your parents handle your disappointment?

______

______

______

7. How do you set yourself up for disappointment?

______

______

______

8. What are your *secondary feelings* about feeling disappointed?

______

______

______

9. Which of your expectations most often lead to your feeling disappointed (for example, needing to succeed, be liked, or be perfect)?

______

______

______

10. How does focusing on food or weight help when you're disappointed?

____

____

____

11. How could you handle disappointment more effectively?

____

____

____

10

Confusion

(To Eat or Not to Eat, That Is the Question!)

You might be wondering why I include confusion as a troublesome emotion for disordered eaters when it seems more like a fuzzy state of mind than a bona fide, bust-you-up feeling. What confusion brings to mind is, perhaps, a grandmother who mixes up her grandchildren's names, or a co-worker who never seems to get instructions right the first time. Perhaps we don't give it weight because it fails to tackle us the way hate, love, anxiety, grief, shame, and guilt do.

Although it may not usher in a blast of affect, confusion nevertheless has a way of making us feel extremely uneasy, unsettled, unfocused, and off balance—*what should we think, which way should we turn, what's right or wrong*? Often we're not even aware that we're caught up in the throes of it! Saying we're tired, overwhelmed, stressed, irritable, in a fog, or out of sorts, we fail to recognize confusion's manifestations and lose out on a valuable learning opportunity.

How do I know if I'm feeling confused?

Confusion actually encompasses a variety of physical/mental/emotional states of "not knowing": *basic confusion, uncertainty, mixed or conflicting feelings, chronic self-doubt,* and *second-guessing.*

Basic Confusion

When you're confused, your thoughts and feelings are jumbled, scrambled, vague, and indecipherable. In a word, you're clueless. Your head may literally ache and your mental processes even may shut down. Symptoms include fatigue, surreal sensations, disorientation, cognitive paralysis, and/or detachment from your thoughts and emotions.

Pure confusion is usually of high intensity, but short-lived. If it persists and a great deal is at stake, you might feel as if you're losing your mind, though that's the opposite of what's actually happening. Letting confusion play itself out gives you a chance to do some genuine problem-solving by pointing you toward options. Sometimes you'll get only a glimmer of recognizable alternatives and at other times, in a "Eureka!" moment, you'll know exactly what to do.

Uncertainty

Uncertainty is far less frenzied than confusion and is generally of low intensity and short duration because there's not a great deal at stake. When you're uncertain, you know what your alternatives are, but have trouble choosing between or among them. Although you might experience mild discomfort being tugged in one direction or another, there's no major emotional attachment or investment in the outcome (which is what often makes choice so doggone difficult): You can swing by to pick up your dry cleaning today or tomorrow, go with Verizon or Comcast, or order that trendy coffee table in cherry, maple, or teak.

Yet chronic, low-intensity uncertainty can undermine and erode self-trust and self-esteem because it makes you feel as if you can't make a decision, even about small things. It may give others the impression that you're passive and indifferent, and can leave you feeling like a wishy-washy individual who isn't willing to take a stand or doesn't much care what happens.

Mixed or Conflicted Feelings

When veins of anxiety run through uncertainty, you've moved on to experiencing mixed or conflicting feelings. You're pulled in opposite directions, as if a boxing match or tug-of-war is raging between your ears. You speculate, "Should I leave my marriage? My job? Have a hip replacement? Bear a child?" You may feel overcome by a sense of inadequacy as well as overwhelmed at having to deal with competing feelings simultaneously, especially if you're ill at ease attending to emotions in general. You may be so full of contradictions that you can't seem to make any decisions at all. When you're feeling unfocused, helpless and irritable, other people may see you as distant or preoccupied.

A hallmark of mixed or conflicting feelings is repeatedly *saying* you want to do one thing, but not *doing* it, or doing its opposite. For example, let's say you're sick of focusing on how much you weigh, but can't quite bring yourself to put away your scale. You've been battling with this dilemma for ages. The problem is that you're in touch with only one set of emotions, the "positive" ones (the pros) telling you that it's a healthy move to ditch the scale. The other set of feelings, which is comprised of your fears (the cons), is hidden out of awareness. When you think about it, there are real reasons you'd be scared to stop weighing yourself: dependence on a number to tell you what and what not to eat, lack of trust that your body can take over the job, fear of getting fat or of no longer being thin.

Conflicting feelings may flare up and die down quickly, last for extended periods, or flicker at a low level throughout your life. You may feel "split in two" about abstractions or concrete, everyday life issues: eating meat, placing your elderly father in a nursing home, your looks, the existence of

God, city living, your relationship with your brother, the meaning of life, or whether killing is ever justified. These issues generally are not in the forefront of your mind every waking minute, but when they pop up, they can cause quite an emotional ruckus.

Though generally unpleasant, holding two opposing views is not necessarily a negative. Some things in life are far too complicated and complex to yield easy answers. If you're conflicted or ambivalent about abstract ideas such as the meaning of life or believing in God, you may be able to tolerate the tension and not pay it much heed. Such is the nature of the well-examined life. At other times, often with more practical matters, you may force yourself to come down on one side or the other for the sole purpose of having peace of mind. The key is to be able to distinguish between which issues can remain unresolved and which can't.

✓ STOP AND FEEL

Are you having mixed feelings right now about working on your eating problems?
If so, what are they?

___

___

___

Chronic Self-Doubt

When it comes to disordered eaters, this particular state of not knowing deserves special mention. If you don't trust your own judgment and lack faith in your decision-making, chances are you're riddled with chronic self-doubt, not only about food, eating, body image, and weight issues, but about other concerns as well. Although it's necessary to reflect on your choices as you make them, constantly cross-examining yourself can be demoralizing and ruin the quality of your life. Having a life-long case of the "doubts" can undermine sound decisions or prevent you from making them. It makes eating and weight issues especially difficult because so much of having a healthy body and mind is predicated on trusting your instincts and your judgment.

✓ STOP AND FEEL

What do you have doubts about right now?

___

___

___

Second-Guessing

All the variations of confusion mentioned so far occur in the present. Second-guessing refers to decisions you've made in the past that still cause you grave concern. You wonder if you hurt someone's feelings by telling the truth, are unsure whether you should have had that tricky knee surgery two years ago, or feel lingering regret about not accepting a marriage proposal from your high school sweetheart. Everyone second-guesses themselves at times—it prevents rigid, perfectionist thinking and promotes honest self-scrutiny and flexible problem-solving. It's healthy to review your decisions in terms of their consequences, but it's unhealthy if you're prone to analyzing and re-analyzing everything you've done in the past day, week, or month—or even throughout your life.

✓ STOP AND FEEL

Are you second-guessing yourself about something right now?

____

____

____

☼ PRACTICE EXERCISE

Charting Consequences

PURPOSE: To anticipate consequences of decision-making

RATIONALE: You may put off making a decision because thinking about its consequences makes you anxious. However, you need to push through discomfort in order to problem-solve effectively.

DIRECTIONS: Pick an ongoing internal conflict that you've been struggling with for a long time—making that doctor's appointment about the lump you found, insisting your adult child move out of the house and get a job, giving up cigarettes, going into therapy, changing jobs—and write about what might happen if you choose each option. For example, if you want to give up cigarettes, write out what you expect your life will be like if you do. Then write about what could happen if you don't give up smoking. Do this exercise with any conflicts for which you have mixed or conflicting feelings.

Conflict #1______________________________

Positive Consequences

____

____

____

Negative Consequences

____

____

____

Conflict #2______________________________________

Positive Consequences

____

____

____

Negative Consequences

____

____

____

REFLECTION (to be done after completion of exercise): It can be very uncomfortable to experience mixed feelings. What was the hardest thing about this exercise? What did you learn about your fears? Is it easier to make a decision now that you understand both sides of your feelings?

____

____

____

The Double Bind

One other kind of confusion deserves mention, the *double bind,* which is a situation in which you can't make a choice because you're trying to respond to two relatively equal, competing, mutually exclusive messages. When you lean toward one, you're ignoring the other, so that choosing feels impossible. This dilemma is called a double bind because the messages are contradictory; you're damned if you do and damned if you don't.

Here are two food-related examples to illustrate this kind of dilemma. Maybe you have an ultra-thin mom who is always on a diet and who also pushs you to clean your plate at every meal. Should you emulate her and aim to be thin, or possibly gain weight by eating when you're full to please her? Or your dad told you he loved you, chubbiness and all, but made snide remarks about your older sisters gaining weight. Should you believe that Dad loves you with a little meat on your bones or that he'd love you more if you took off a few pounds? Because you want to *be* like your parents as well as be *liked* by them, the contradictions in these two situations make a choice impossible.

Double messages about weight and food abound in society—eat foods that aren't good for you because they're delicious, but don't get fat. Your body is your own, but say "Yes" or "No" to food just to spare someone else hurt feelings. Love your body, but only if it looks like a model's. Be your natural self, but look like a million bucks all the time. As you can see, double binds can have you chasing your tail.

Some of the most difficult double binds are those that pit your internal messages against external ones: you've eaten enough and someone you love says you should eat more or should have eaten less. You like comfortable, loose clothing, but your boyfriend urges you to dress in skin-tight jeans. You're hungry for real food, but all your friends are on a new fad diet. The only constructive way out of a double bind is to ignore the unhealthy message, choose the healthy one, and go for it. A good place to start is to identify your double binds around food and weight.

☼ PRACTICE EXERCISE

Double Messages and Double Binds

PURPOSE: To identify double messages from your family and the general culture which lead to double binds about eating and weight

RATIONALE: In order to avoid the damage of double messages, we need to be aware of them and of the conflict they create in us.

DIRECTIONS: Below, write the opposing messages you received in childhood or from society about food, eating, weight, or your body. A family example might say, "Clean your plate" and "Don't get fat." A societal example might be, "You can never be too thin" and "Thin means being seen as sexual." Come up with as many conflicting messages as you can and relate them to the current binds you're stuck in, such as both wanting and fearing weight gain, trying to please someone by eating or not eating, wishing to be a perfect "eater" and knowing there's no such thing. Then write down how to get out of the bind.

Double Bind #1________________________________

Message____

____

Opposing message__________________________________

____

Healthy resolution__________________________________

____

Double Bind #2______________________________________

Message____

____

Opposing message____

____

Healthy resolution ____

____

REFLECTION (to be done after completion of exercise): Can you see the connection between mixed messages and your double binds? It should help a great deal to put them to paper so you can recognize both how pulled apart and how stuck you are. What did you do to resolve your binds in a healthy way?

____

____

____

Why is confusion so difficult to tolerate?

Many of my clients consider confusion (and its brethren) a negative thing and you may agree. Here's why. First and foremost, we live in a culture that, unfortunately, idealizes and encourages simplistic thinking. Make things too complicated and most people get twitchy, glaze over and give up. Give us "yes" or "no," good or evil, saint or sinner, right or wrong. Critical thinking? Ambiguity? Ambivalence? Forget it. So *when there's no quick-and-easy answer, people erroneously believe that something must be wrong*. However, life isn't like making instant soup—follow the directions and pronto, grab a spoon. Life is big and bewildering, complicated and contradictory, mysterious and mystifying—in short, anything but simple.

Another reason you might devalue the state of not knowing is that it's definitely unpleasant and hard to tolerate—too many sensations striking your gong at once. In response, to rid yourself of inner tension, you may try to force a solution. Or, convinced that thinking about a subject will tear you apart or overwhelm you, you may keep tucking it out of awareness for peace of mind.

Perhaps most importantly, not knowing causes discomfort because you feel you *ought* to know, *should* be able to decide, and *must* come up with an answer. You may believe that other people never feel confused or conflicted, and that something is seriously wrong with you for not having a snap solution at your fingertips. Ironically, the more desperate you are for certainty and the more pressure you put on yourself for answers, the more elusive they often remain.

✓ STOP AND FEEL

What are you feeling right now?

____

____

____

What is the purpose of confusion?

The purpose of confusion, uncertainty and mixed emotions is to provide an opportunity to process information in order to make conscious, healthy choices. Without confusion and mixed feelings, your mind would be set and rigid—a room with a closed door and no open windows. Not knowing brings in a breath of fresh air (okay, sometimes a stiff breeze or even a gale-force hurricane) and keeps it circulating. If you're never confused, uncertain or self-doubting, you'll never grow and change; instead you'll remain stuck, stagnant, and emotionally barricaded. Confusion may be exactly what you need to rearrange the clutter in your mind (or life).

Let's run through an example from confusion to possible resolution to see how difficult yet beneficial tolerating not knowing can be. The process needs to be organic, meaning that it should evolve naturally from within you. It requires patience for it to move along on its own timetable (not the one you want to impose on it!).

Say you're not sure if you should stay with your spouse—an issue that crops up frequently in my psychotherapy practice. At first, you have only the vague sensation that things aren't quite right between you, or could be better. This feeling subsides, but never completely disappears. Label these stirrings confusion—a jumble of insights, reactions, impressions, and perceptions. So far, you're feeling mildly concerned, okay as long as your feelings don't intensify.

> ***Confusion may be exactly what you need to rearrange the clutter in your mind (or life).***

Next, you start to notice more and more things you dislike about your spouse—he's messy, she's prissy, he's rude to your friends, she never wants to go anywhere. Now you're moving into a mild state of ambivalence or mixed feelings. You may be shocked or upset that you're entertaining negative feelings and want to push them away. They may disappear for a while, then return. Something's not right, but nothing's terribly wrong either. There's still more "Yes" than "No" in the marriage.

If you stay with these authentic, disturbing feelings long enough, you'll eventually move to a state which is highly conflicted and agitating. You'll be uncertain whether to stay or go because there'll be reasons to stick around and equally compelling ones to catch the next coach out of Dodge. Feeling conflicted is a terribly uncomfortable sensation. I can't say this often enough. You're split in two, ripped apart, particularly as the pressure—internal and external—to arrive at a decision mounts. Moreover, you'll probably have feelings *about* your feelings: you *should* be able to make a decision, there's something wrong if you can't, you're a coward or looking for trouble, you're taking too long to make up your mind or should quit rocking the boat.

Playing out this marital scenario, eventually you'll make a decision to stay or to go or you'll make no conscious choice and thereby fall back to the status quo of remaining conflicted. If you make a clear decision (to enter counseling and try to work things out, or to leave immediately and get your own apartment), you've been through a process, a healthy, normal, natural progression that has taken you to a new place, from vague uneasiness to clarity (albeit, probably with reservations). Even if you decide to stay with your spouse, you're in a different place than you were when you noticed your first flicker of conjugal unease.

How does fear play a part in confusion?

Unresolved internal conflict, chronic self-doubt, and second-guessing are all based on fear of consequences. Here's what happens. Say you've been struggling for months about whether to say something to your boss about how abusively he treats you. Underneath your confusion, you're really afraid of the price you may pay for speaking up. Similarly, if you've been telling yourself and your friends for years that you're going to return to grad school, but never pick up a catalogue, you're harboring reservations, perhaps about flunking out, overburdening yourself, or going into further debt.

> *Being afraid of how choices will play out and come back to haunt you prevents you from committing to a course of action.*

Or you may second-guess decisions you've already made. Say you finally mustered your courage and spoke up to that boss of yours about how he humiliates and yells at you in front of your co-workers, and now he barely utters a word in your direction except to give you work assignments. You may be afraid that you went too far and that his anger will boil over and he'll fire you. Or maybe you finally got into grad school, and are now overwhelmed with doubt every time you receive a new homework assignment. You know you have to get the work done, but have so little time with work and family obligations, that you often consider dropping out. Both reactions come from your underlying fear of having made a mistake.

I assure you, you didn't come to be afraid of being wrong or failing on your own. The way your family made choices, lived with their consequences, and what they taught you about decision-making shaped how you make them today. If you were encouraged through childhood and adolescence to think for yourself and learn from your mistakes, you probably matured into a person who's not terribly afraid to be wrong or fail and who figures you'll be right and successful at least as often as not. You won't need to be right all the time and won't care all that much if you're wrong. You'll take measured risks and live reasonably well with their consequences.

However, if you grew up in a household where one or both parents *had* to be right, there's a good chance you experienced or witnessed a great deal of arguing, quibbling, sniping, and perhaps even verbal abuse. You lacked the freedom to explore your own thinking and come to your own conclusions through trial and error because you had to toe the line—or else. If your opinions or actions were regularly undermined, criticized, or demeaned, you may have come to believe that they're not worth a dime, that you can't trust your judgment, and that you're inept at making decisions. Now, you may fear voicing opinions, or even having them. Your silence not only paralyzes your tongue, but numbs your brain and your heart.

If your parents insisted on making decisions for you, even when you were old enough to make them yourself, you may have concluded that you're incapable of sorting out and making good choices. Your fear of making mistakes may cause you to look to people to decide for you, even while you resent others for usurping your rightful power. You're stuck between wanting and hating to be dependent, wishing to be more resourceful on your own and fearing that you'll fail.

Your parents may have employed a hands-off attitude and rarely, if ever, helped guide you. Maybe they believed they shouldn't intrude, didn't have a clue what was best for you, or didn't care. Perhaps they were afraid of influencing you, being wrong, or being blamed. Whatever the reason, without sound age-appropriate guidance, you may have felt overwhelmed with choices too early in life. Today, though you know your judgment isn't always sound, you still may be afraid to seek advice, leaving you struggling with your difficulties alone.

Remember, you'll only develop self-trust and confidence by making your own decisions, learning from mistakes, and by doing what's in your best interest and makes you proud.

✓ STOP AND FEEL

How do you feel about what you learned in childhood about trusting yourself and making decisions? How do you feel about trusting others to help you?

____

____

____

BELIEFS ABOUT CONFUSION

Because rational thinking leads to rational behavior, it's essential that you build a belief-system that's sound and healthy. Here are examples of irrational thoughts turned into rational ones.

IB: Feeling confused means there's something wrong with me.
RB: Feeling confused is normal and means I need more information or time to make up my mind.

IB: If I was smarter or more secure, I wouldn't feel confused.
RB: Everyone feels confused sometimes.

IB: I should always know what I want.
RB: Sometimes it's not possible to know right away what I want.
RB: Sometimes important decisions take time.

IB: I should never have self doubt.
RB: Having occasional self doubt is normal and healthy.

IB: I can't bear feeling confused.
RB: I can bear feeling confused and any other feeling.
RB: By bearing confusion, I'll find a good solution.

IB: Strong people aren't indecisive.
RB: Strong people make informed decisions which may take time.

IB: I have to make the right decisions so I won't make mistakes or fail.
RB: Failure and mistakes are part of life.
IB: I'm allowed to make mistakes and fail.

IB: Mixed feelings mean I'm wishy washy.
RB: Mixed feelings are natural and a sign I'm not rigid and simplistic.

Now it's your turn to transform your irrational beliefs into sound, functional ones. Take your time and make sure each new, rational belief feels right for you. They should be concrete and written in the present tense using an active verb. Feel free to use the list above, but make sure you come up with some of your own as well.

Irrational Belief	Rational Belief
____________________	____________________
____________________	____________________
____________________	____________________
____________________	____________________

How is confusion related to my problems with food and weight?

When you're unhappy and uncomfortable that you don't have the answers you want, fixating on food or weight is a welcome distraction. Changing your focus brings immediate relief from the fireworks or paralysis inside. If you're in the midst of a pitched emotional battle about whether to move halfway around the world to join your lover, a bowl of munchies is a perfect time-out to help you chew things over! When you can't decide if you should drive down to visit your parents for the weekend because you always return home angry and depressed, what better moment to have a seat and meticulously plan out every morsel you'll eat for the next week.

So much of life has unknowable, unpredictable outcomes that you may feel condemned to waffle in your mind forever—*should I take the cushy job or the one where I can really make a difference? Should I visit my self-centered sister in the hospital or go out with friends? Should I have a colonoscopy as my doctor insists or put it off for another year?* When you spend too much time agonizing over difficult decisions, focusing on whether or what to eat grounds you in your body. After all, there's nothing iffy about food; it's about as concrete and solid as you can get. Compared to deciding life's serious issues, food is a piece of cake!

Compared to deciding life's serious issues, food is a piece of cake!

Moreover, after you're done obsessing, eating, weighing yourself, throwing out all the "fattening" food in your kitchen, or any other food-related activity, there's a good chance you're not going to be feeling too great about yourself. And when that happens, all the *agita* that caused your diversion in the first place will be replaced by guilt, shame, self-loathing, and remorse, the familiar emotions that come rushing in when you've acted out impulsively rather than tackled problems head on.

Another reason you act out in the food arena is that so many of your dilemmas are about food and weight. When you're cut off from your hidden feelings about eating and your body, you can't help but continue to play them out through destructive behavior. Well, that behavior is struggling to tell you something by trying to reveal the fears you've been unwilling or unable to see.

For instance, you insist you really want to put on weight, but are unaware how truly frightened you are to give up the one thing you believe makes you special—your thinness. So you keep finding excuses to not eat. Or you commit to stop eating when you're full, but are disconnected from how your impoverished childhood has left you feeling deprived and hating to say "No" to yourself. The underbelly of your feelings prevents you from stopping, and once again, you overeat. *The fact is, when negative feelings remain out of consciousness, they find a way to break through and surface in your behavior.* While you focus on what you want, your behavior is playing out what you don't want. This behavior is often called "leaking" or "acting out." The only prevention is to troll deep for the "cons" you're feeling as well as the "pros."

If you continue to run away from the confusion of not knowing what to do, you're missing out on a vital process which will only help you move forward successfully through life. Sure it's uncomfortable not to have answers, to take risks and fail, to wonder if you're wrong, to make mistakes and live with undesirable consequences. But if you're not willing to struggle through the fog, how will you ever find your way out to sunshine and blue sky?

FURTHER EXPLORATION

1. How do you know when you're feeling confused or conflicted?

2. What are your *secondary feelings* about not knowing?

3. When you were a child, how did your parents deal with *their* confusion, mixed feelings, or doubts?

4. When you were a child, how did your parents deal with *yours*?

5. How does focusing on food or weight serve you when you don't know what to do, feel torn, or can't make up your mind?

6. If you suffer from chronic self-doubt or second-guessing yourself, how could you become more self-trusting and confident?

7. What double messages did you receive about emotions growing up, particularly about eating and your body?

8. What are your double binds about your food and weight?

9. How could you deal with confusion, uncertainty, and mixed or conflicting feelings more effectively?

11

Loneliness

(Table for One, Please!)

Perhaps Noah loaded his ship two by two not only to ensure preservation of the species, but also because he understood how much living things crave companionship and connection. We all need to carve out time for ourselves, but the fact is, it's natural to get lonely for what people have to offer: empathy, comfort, validation, conversation, respect, amusement, mature love, stimulation, exchange of ideas, wisdom, feedback, a sense of mutual purpose, a mirror in which we can see ourselves clearly.

Of course, some of these needs can be met in other ways. You and your Lab can join a volunteer rescue team and share a mutual purpose, you can amuse yourself watching TV or playing computer games, feel joy harvesting fresh vegetables from your fall garden, or gain wisdom by reading the classics. However, nowhere else can you get the whole package but in another human being.

Loneliness is vastly different than being alone by choice. Solitude can bring peace of mind and a quiet joy and contentment. It can refresh and revitalize the spirit by re-engaging us with ourselves, with nature, and with our private passions. The pain of loneliness, however, springs from a darker place because separateness and disconnection are not of our choosing.

How do I know if I'm feeling lonely?

Loneliness, more than some other emotions, has a strong physical component. You may feel heavy or leaden, listless, hollow, bored, or antsy. You may have a sense of being isolated, apart, and excluded, even experiencing a surreal sense of being on the outside looking in. Loneliness is a feeling of discontent about disconnection and aloneness, an ache for human contact. It's not related to the number of people in a room or in your life, and is as much about depth of attachment as breadth of connection.

Isolation and disconnection can be intensely depressing, and are often accompanied by feeling unwanted, unneeded, invisible, sad, abandoned, rejected, and helpless. The belief that you are unloved and unlovable can be such a strong undercurrent through loneliness that it strikes at the very core of your self-esteem. Feeling worthless, hopeless, and set apart from the human race, you might wish you'd never been born or even want to die.

✓ STOP AND FEEL

What are you feeling right now?

____

____

____

What is the purpose of loneliness?

Loneliness is pretty simple and straightforward and lets you know that you want people in your life. If chronic, it can reveal a disappointing scarcity of relationships or expose the shallowness of your so-called friendships. Pangs of loneliness may also be a testament to the deep attachments you have and miss.

Although feeling lonely directs you toward people, you may have to dig deeper for answers to find exactly what you're lonely for. For example, maybe you have lots of friends with whom to go to movies, shows, sports events, and out to dinner, but only one or two with whom you can truly have a heart-to-heart. In this case, loneliness is telling you that you want less activity and more intimacy. On the other hand, perhaps you have three or four friends with whom you can bare your soul, but none who like to roller skate, ski, play chess, bargain hunt at flea markets, or take in a baseball game. In this case, loneliness is pushing you to get out there and find people who will share your passions.

What factors influence my experience of loneliness?

In spite of the fact that feeling lonely is a universal emotion, nature and nurture both play a part in determining how we experience it. Below are primary contributors.

Biology

The desire to attach is hard-wired into humans. Parents have an innate desire to care for their offspring and children have an equal, inborn need to seek care. Once again, nature is at work making sure the human race survives and flourishes.

However, attachment is not a one-size-fits-all dynamic. Infants exhibit varying needs for attachment and closeness. Some crave touch, adore being coddled, and can't bear to be apart from their caretakers, while others cry the minute they're picked up or fussed over, but burble happily when left to their own devices. Even when they're barely out of the womb, some newborns appear to suffer markedly less from being left alone than others. Down the road, our biological inclination interacts with our upbringing to determine our interest in and tolerance for attachment.

Parent-Child Attachment

We have to slip into rewind mode to understand another significant contributor to our experience of loneliness: early attachment to our parents. We're born through connection, initially through joining of sperm and egg, and then through adherence of the fetus to Mother's body. Even when this concrete bond is severed by birth, we're still tightly tied to parents by our physical and emotional dependence on them. Healthy attachments early on are crucial to development. Without them as infants and children, we would die. Without them as adults, we may suffer overwhelming chronic or pervasive loneliness.

Healthy attachments early on are crucial to development.

Let's look at how healthy attachments are formed. When parents model a spousal relationship that includes a reasonable balance of closeness and distance and when they provide us with a similar mix, we learn that we can have people in our lives when we want them and also can be alone when we need to be. If the bond with our parents is basically sound, we're comfortable letting it slacken and are able to go on to form affiliations with relatives, friends, teachers, and neighbors.

As time passes, many of these relationships end and we develop new ones, which teaches us that life is an endless series of connections and disconnections, attachments and detachments. When separations occur, we're not frightened because we've developed inner resources to cope with our feelings, and also assume that if we keep reaching out, someone will eventually be there for us. In adulthood, we will feel lonely occasionally, but it won't cause excessive distress.

However, the process of early attachment doesn't always go well, which may set the stage for negative experiences with people and consequent loneliness in adulthood. Sometimes our primary caretaker, usually Mother, is unable to give us what we need in infancy and childhood and healthy bonding with her is difficult or impossible. For a variety of reasons, she may be distant or overly intrusive, or an unpredictable, arbitrary combination of the two. Or a parent may have a lengthy illness or die when we are very young. Grief stricken, we may be scared to form relationships because of the pain of losing them. Unable to satisfactorily attach and, later, separate appropriately, we may become clingy and/or withdrawn when our needs are not adequately met.

Parent-Parent Attachment

Earlier, I mentioned that when parents display an appropriate balance of closeness and distance with a spouse, we learn the meaning of healthy self-regulation in a relationship: sometimes people (even spouses) want to be close and sometimes they don't. Sadly, many parents have trouble with intimacy and are unable to provide a healthy model. One way the relationship malfunctions is when parents have little or no physical contact with each other, barely speak about personal matters, or basically function in separate orbits and don't appear to notice or mind. Such disengagement teaches us that people don't need people and that getting close is wrong or unnatural.

Another way we end up with faulty assumptions about intimacy is when parents are overly involved and enmeshed, such as when they constantly speak for each other and refuse to spend a moment apart. From this we learn that people must be in each other's pocket or something's amiss. With either dysfunctional dynamic, we develop unhealthy beliefs that later contribute to our adult expectations about relationships and leave us feeling lonely. Either we yearn for closeness but don't feel it's our right and often sabotage ourselves when we do connect, or we push people away in fear of needing them and end up being overwhelmed by our needs when we try to handle them alone.

It's easy to see how inadequate early attachment and poor modeling of intimacy can lead to ignorance about and fear of connection. Because of our upbringing, we may not have learned the skills for connecting or even recognize its tremendous value. Although desperate to have people in our lives, we may not know how to start or keep relationships, leaving us frustrated and lonely. Or we may deny a need for intimacy and pretend we're fine without it, which only means we're unaware of our loneliness, not that it doesn't drive us in unhealthy ways.

Disconnection from Self

Another contributor to loneliness stems from a disconnection from authentic self. If parents are disconnected from their needs and emotions, they can't teach us how to connect to ours. Nor can they model how to act positively and proactively when we feel vulnerable because of our yearnings; instead, we get the message to protect the inner self at all cost. When we learn early on to cut off or shut down feelings, to distract ourselves from them, or pretend they aren't there, we eventually become emotionally numb. Just as we have to love ourselves before we can love other people, we have to be connected to ourselves—to our authentic emotions—before we can connect intimately with others. In this case, the cause of loneliness is not isolation from other people or withdrawal of companionship or affection, but our distance from ourselves and what we feel.

Another contributor to loneliness stems from a disconnection from authentic self.

Inclusion and Exclusion

A sense of being excluded can strongly contribute to the pain of loneliness. We learn about inclusion and exclusion in our first group experience with our family of origin. When as children we feel loved, valued, and included, loneliness is an infrequent and fleeting feeling. When it visits, we have only to remember that warm, fuzzy sensation of being part of a loving group, and the insecurity disappears. In this way, a strong sense of belonging plays a large part in driving away loneliness.

If, however, there were cliques or unequal attentions given within the family, we probably cued in to them fairly quickly. For example, when parents of necessity (due to health or other reasons) need to give special attention to one child at the expense of another, it's natural for the non-special child to feel hurt or left out. Or when all four boys in a household run off to play, leaving their sister behind. Or when three older siblings lose patience and refuse to include the "baby" of the family in their games. As children, we're not thinking rationally about the situation: we just know that our needs got shelved. When parents are sensitive to our needs, they can minimize our hurt and disappointment by helping us deal with them. When they're not tuned in, however, we end up feeling angry, resentful, too needy, undeserving, or depressed.

We also become sensitized to inclusion and exclusion in our second significant group experience—school. Each one of us wants to be part of the in-crowd and dreads feeling like an outsider. If we're lucky enough to feel a sense of belonging in school, as well as a firm sense of individuality and self-sufficiency, we aren't likely to experience prolonged loneliness. However, if we're picked on, teased, labeled, or repeatedly left out when we want in, we may finally give up, choosing to feel lonely over humiliated and rejected. This kind of formative experience can take a long time and a great deal of effort to sort out and overcome. When that doesn't happen, we end up in adulthood with our noses pressed against the window, forever looking out.

✓ STOP AND FEEL

When you stop and pay attention to how connected you are to yourself and other people, what do you feel?

____

____

____

☼ PRACTICE EXERCISE

UNDERSTANDING FAMILY CONNECTIONS

PURPOSE: To recognize the strength of connections among family members

RATIONALE: The dynamics we experience in our family of origin provide the blueprint for how we react to people later in life. A good start in dealing with your loneliness is to understand its origin.

DIRECTIONS: On the next page, you'll be drawing a chart of the family in which you grew up, including your parents, siblings, and close relatives. Write your name under the stick figure in the center of the diagram. Next, you will draw stick figures representing the other people, including their names. Make the people you feel closest to nearest to the stick figure of you.

____

Your Name

REFLECTION (to be done after completion of exercise): What did you notice about closeness in your family? By examining your diagram, you should see a schema of the kind of connections (or lack thereof) you experienced growing up. How do they affect your sense of loneliness today?

____

____

____

Is feeling lonely the same as feeling bored or empty?

Many people confuse being lonely with being bored. When you're bored, you ache to *do something* and the cure is activity. When you're lonely, you long to *be with someone* and the solution is people. You may even experience these two emotions in tandem. When this happens, the only way you'll know whether you're yearning for people or action is to stop and take a minute to tap into your needs.

Moreover, emptiness, a painful affect that is strikingly prevalent among people with eating problems, is often mistaken for loneliness. Feelings of emptiness occur when you either disconnect from your deepest longings and desires or have not found ways to meet them, leaving you rarely, if ever, feeling "full-filled." You may be afraid to discover or acknowledge your desires because you'll fail to reach them or because you think you're not worthy of them. You may be put off by the time and patience it takes to get to know yourself and to recognize what pleases you and what doesn't. You may even believe that if you start to uncover your needs, you'll feel greedy and want more than you can ever get.

When you're cut off from authentic feeling, you don't really know what you're empty *for* and may fall prey to society's quick fixes—filling up on possessions, excitement, substances, recognition, or physical perfection (whatever *that* is!). You may believe that if you have enough clothes, cars, books, CDs, vacations, children, bling, compliments, club memberships, or food that you'll finally feeling content and complete. However, trying to fill up solely on these kinds of externals is like topping off a leaky bucket—the faster you pour in the water, the faster it seeps out the other end.

> *Lasting, meaningful fulfillment comes only from acknowledging and experiencing emptiness and letting it point you toward what would fill you up.*

The solution to emptiness may be engaging work or a sense of higher purpose; often it's creativity and challenge. Taking the time to explore emptiness, painful as it is, will lead you to the unique experiences that will bring you a sense of satisfaction and fullness.

Disconnecting from authentic feelings is only one avenue that leads to emptiness. The other is knowing what would float your boat, but doing nothing about it. You may feel deeply unsatisfied because you're an accountant, not an aviator, because you've always wanted children but are childless, or because you're afraid that novel you've been dying to write won't get finished. You'll continue to feel empty by refusing to follow what's in your heart. If you suffer from chronic emptiness, maybe now is the time to uncork the bottle, and see what comes out. You can't fill yourself up if you don't know what you lack!

Can I avoid loneliness?

Some amount of loneliness is unavoidable and part of the human condition. Everyone has pangs of it now and then. One person might experience only an occasional hankering for human contact, while another might seek companionship almost 24/7, while yet a third might yearn for friendship but also find it suffocating and, therefore, make do with loose, sporadic connections.

The degree of loneliness people feel is partially dependent on what drives them. Some are highly inner-directed, getting their juice from within, while others are highly outer-directed and get energized from being with people. Most are a mix and enjoy solo periods as much as socializing. There's neither a right nor a wrong in being one kind of person or the other, and each develops from a combination of nature and nurture. However, all things being equal, it makes sense that inner-directed people are less likely than outer-directed people to suffer from extreme loneliness.

Moreover, people are lonely for a variety of reasons. Sometimes the cause is situational: they've just lost their mate of 50 years, they're new to an area, or the last of their children has just left the nest. Other people endure a deeper, more chronic and lingering loneliness that gets woven into the fabric of their lives. They keep to themselves, have few, or no, real friendships, and do most activities alone. Even when they're with people, they feel set apart and experience a social awkwardness and alienation that prevent them from making intimate connections. Obviously, this kind of loneliness is more profound and painful than the more transitory, situational kind.

BELIEFS ABOUT LONELINESS

Because rational thinking leads to rational behavior, building a belief-system that's sound and healthy is essential. Here are examples of irrational thoughts turned into rational ones.

IB: I can't bear feeling lonely.
RB: I can bear feeling lonely and any other feelings.

IB: When I'm lonely, focusing on food is the only thing that makes me feel better.
RB: When I'm lonely, there are many ways I can feel better that don't relate to food.

IB: I don't need people in my life.
RB: Everyone needs people in their life to greater or lesser extent.

IB: I always pick the wrong people and end up lonely, so why bother?
RB: There are wonderful people out there who will love and want to be with me.

IB: I should never be lonely.
RB: Everyone is lonely once in a while.

IB: When I'm lonely I have to find people to be with.
RB: Sometimes people are the answer to my loneliness and sometimes they're not.
RB: Learning to enjoy myself by myself will help me feel less lonely.

IB: Food is a good friend.
RB: Food is a poor substitute for good friends.

Now it's your turn to transform your irrational beliefs into sound, functional ones. Take your time and make sure each new, rational belief feels right for you. They should be concrete and written in the present tense using an active verb. Feel free to use the list on the previous page, but make sure you come up with some of your own as well.

Irrational Belief	Rational Belief
______________________________	______________________________
______________________________	______________________________
______________________________	______________________________
______________________________	______________________________

☼ PRACTICE EXERCISE

What Am I Really Feeling?

PURPOSE: To recognize the difference between boredom, emptiness, and loneliness

RATIONALE: Confusing loneliness, emptiness, and boredom makes it difficult to find a solution to eliminate or lessen the feeling. When you know exactly what you feel, an appropriate response is easier to find.

DIRECTIONS: Use the chart below to compare and contrast the differences between loneliness, boredom, and emptiness. Think about the last time you felt each of these feelings. For example, for a Physical Manifestation of lonely you might put "crying." Under Thoughts Were About, you might say "old boyfriend." A Solution might be "call best friend."

	Physical manifestation	*Thoughts were about*	*Solution might be*
Lonely –			
Bored –			
Empty –			

REFLECTION (to be done after completion of exercise): Do loneliness, boredom, and emptiness, manifest themselves physically in the same way or differently? When you're bored, do you often feel empty as well? Are there times when you may feel all three emotions at once?

____

____

____

Is keeping busy a good cure for loneliness?

Many people believe that keeping busy will keep loneliness at bay, but this is not always the case. If you've just moved from Boston to Sarasota and don't know a soul, getting out and going for a walk on the beach by yourself or taking in a movie is certainly healthier than sitting in your condo every weekend flipping cable channels. The same is true if you're lonely on a business trip or in a situation where you lack your usual routines, comforts, and connections. When loneliness is temporary, transitory, and circumstantial, staying busy can keep your mind off how much you miss your family or friends, your home, work, or even your old life. Finding interesting and engaging things to do on your own fosters adaptability, reinforces confidence and self-esteem, and helps you feel less lonely. Getting out and being active is also a great way to make new connections.

> ***Maybe you're scared to be by yourself because it means being with yourself.***

On the other hand, in these transitory situations, what's wrong with feeling a little blue? Isn't your lonesomeness a testament to the firm attachments you've made? If you believe you need to eradicate all your lonely feelings or you'll become depressed, maybe you've never really been on your own and miss familiar attachments so much that you're at loose ends. Maybe you're scared to be by yourself because it means being *with* yourself. Or perhaps you've become so reliant on being with people that you only know who you are in relation to them and need to fly solo for a while to become acquainted with the real you.

If your loneliness is pervasive and ongoing, you may use structure and activity as a distraction from pain. In fact, you may be addicted to busyness as a way of coping. If so, you're short-changing yourself—compulsively being on the go will always be a poor substitute for genuine intimacy, authentic self-reliance, being still, and experiencing your feelings. When relationships are abundant and meaningful *and* you also enjoy being alone, you can stop racing around trying to fill up on mindless activity. The true antidote to loneliness is a healthy combination of strong internal resources and people in your life whom you love and who love you.

☼ PRACTICE EXERCISE

Your Deepest Wish

PURPOSE: To connect with your deepest yearnings, longings, and desires

RATIONALE: You can't find happiness unless you dig deeply through your fears and inhibitions to find out exactly what you yearn for.

WHAT YOU NEED: time and patience

DIRECTIONS: Find a comfortable position. Breathe deeply for 3-5 minutes, until your mind is still and your body feels relaxed. When you're ready, pose this question to yourself: *What do I need to be fulfilled?* Wait for an answer to surface and sit with it for a moment without judging it. Don't rush. Then ask again: *What do I need to be fulfilled?* Once more, be patient and wait for an answer. Keep gently asking the question until you find a response that resonates and is at the core of your wants and needs. For example, your first answer may be "to get married," your second, "to have someone who cares about me," and your final, "to care more about myself." If you can't find an answer right now, don't judge yourself. Simply return to this exercise at another time.

What was your final answer?____

REFLECTION (to be done after completion of exercise): This exercise may be difficult, especially if you're impatient, so switch off the pressure. You'll know you've hit on the "right" answer when you feel a rush or click of emotion that says, "Yes, that's it!" Were you able to continue asking the question until you hit on a response that rang truer than others? What was your reaction to your final answer? If you weren't able to find a "true" answer, why do you think you couldn't?

____

____

____

How does feeling lonely or empty drive me to focus on food?

A focus on food to dull your pain and fill you up might seem a natural response to loneliness or emptiness. Obsessing about food, micromanaging your intake, and compulsive/emotional eating are all distractions from your unknown and unmet longings. *These activities seduce you into feeling focused, engaged, and productive through goal-oriented mental and physical activity.* After all, you're doing *something* when you're counting the calories you plan to eat tomorrow or the ones you ate today; you're full of energy when you're shopping and cooking and making choices in preparation for a binge.

Also, when you're lonely, fixating on food may feel safer than reaching out to friends or trying to make new ones; when you feel empty inside, a food obsession gives you a seemingly worthwhile internal goal. These activities are far easier than creating a network of people to enjoy and be close with, less risky than building a self that's brimming with achievement, integrity, curiosity, generosity, esteem, creativity, and delight.

Unwanted eating is a way to top yourself off, but will always leave you feeling empty and unsatisfied. The same is true of trying to fill yourself up with pride for your thinness and self-restraint. *Moreover, by using inappropriate and self-destructive ways to quell loneliness and emptiness, you reinforce an addiction to unhealthy behaviors and miss out on opportunities for genuine connection and a true sense of fulfillment.*

Sadly, you may believe that food is a more trustworthy companion than any person you've ever met. Having no needs of its own, what could be more predictable and at your service? People may disappoint you, but food always welcomes you with open arms. People may reject you, but food, never! It makes you feel warm inside and sweetens the hours. It may remind you of meals enjoyed with family, or even the closeness you experienced during your first feedings.

On the other hand, denying your hunger may be a metaphor for renouncing all of your needs. You may believe (or want to believe) that if you can say "No" to food, you can ignore your longings for friendship, your desire to succeed, your yearning for happiness, your craving for whatever makes your heart sing. By rejecting food, you're trying to convince yourself that you don't need much. By conquering your physical hunger, you're trying to believe you can triumph over the hungers of your heart as well.

Focusing on food may seem tailor-made for your loneliest hours, but deep down you know you've chosen an activity long on promise and short on substance. You deserve far better. In order to find out what's missing, though, you'll have to suffer the pain of loneliness and emptiness first. And then you'll have to find the strength and courage to go out and pursue your desires. Think of all the energy you put into food obsessions and how wonderful you'd feel putting that amount of effort into building up your self-esteem, developing true friendships, making a better world, and creating a life for yourself that is filled with passion and productivity.

FURTHER EXPLORATION

1. What are the body sensations that tell you you're feeling lonely?

____

____

____

2. How would you describe the purpose of loneliness?

____

____

____

3. What are your *secondary feelings* about being lonely?

____

____

____

4. Describe your family dynamics in terms of connectedness, attachment, privacy, intimacy, inclusion and exclusion?

____

____

____

5. As a child, how did you handle feeling lonely or excluded?

6. If you feel empty as well as lonely, what are you empty for?

7. When you're alone and still, which feelings surface and frighten you?

8. What are the unhealthy non-food ways, such as enforced busyness, that you use to avoid feeling lonely or empty?

9. What do you get out of focusing on food when you feel lonely or empty?

10. Why are you so afraid to seek out people when you're lonely?

11. How could you handle loneliness and emptiness more effectively?

____

____

____

12

Freeing Your Feelings

(Can't I Put 'Em Out With the Trash?)

I hope by now you're convinced that getting to know your emotions is what will move you away from a food obsession and toward a more genuinely fulfilling life. Of course, the idea of allowing your emotions to visit and guide you may still be frightening. If you let down your guard, will they get you into a world of trouble? What if you become so depressed that you can't function? What if you can't shut off your feelings once they start?

Perhaps you fear relying too much on emotions and still think that all you need is a good head on your shoulders to get you through. Fortunately, you don't have to choose *between* judgment and emotion because they're designed to complement each other and work hand in hand. For instance, you can be wary of a family member who hasn't been there for you and still decide to give her another chance. You can grieve the loss of a loved one and still push yourself to keep up with social engagements because you recognize the importance of support. You can feel guilty for hurting a friend while reminding yourself there's no need to keep apologizing for the rest of your life.

Being emotionally healthy means using clear thinking and experiencing a full range of feelings. If you live only by intellect and cognitive powers—the rational mind—life can become a one-note grind. However, if you live solely by your heart, you may not survive long enough to enjoy a full life! Judgment or emotion—neither is better nor worse than the other; they're *value neutral.* Emotion tempered by judgment is the winning recipe!

How can I learn to become comfortable with my feelings?

A good place to start is by examining your beliefs about emotions to ensure that they're sound and healthy. If you still believe that you don't need to listen to your feelings, that it's okay to sidestep or minimize them, that they're something to fear rather than trust, or that you can't bear affective pain, you're not ready to begin taking down the walls you've built around your heart. Irrational, unhealthy beliefs act like sentries, barring you from opening up to your emotions, while rational, healthy beliefs lay out the welcome mat and say, *It's okay, come on in.*

In *Chapter 2: Fear of Feelings,* you made a list of rational and irrational beliefs about emotions. Take a look at them now. Do you have new ones as you near the end of this book? Use the space below to add to or rewrite your rational beliefs, making sure that they are not only rational but also functional. These are the blueprint for putting your emotional house in order.

RATIONAL BELIEFS ABOUT EMOTIONS

1. ______________________________
2. ______________________________
3. ______________________________
4. ______________________________
5. ______________________________
6. ______________________________

The next step is to convert this blueprint into specific instructions for handling your feelings on a daily basis. An *Emotional Do & Don't List* will help. Here's what one might look like.

EMOTIONAL DO & DON'T LISTS

Do...

- allow myself to be vulnerable with people I trust
- fully experience every emotion
- be open and accepting of all my emotions
- be curious rather than judgmental about my emotions
- use people to comfort me when I feel badly, instead of focusing on food
- let my emotions come and go as they please without fear
- populate my inner circle with intimates who are emotionally mature and healthy
- take my time and figure out exactly what I'm feeling
- use my feelings along with my judgment to help me reach my goals, eating and otherwise

Don't...

- pretend I don't feel anything when I do
- ignore or minimize painful feelings
- believe that anyone knows better than I do what I'm feeling
- let people shame or humiliate me for having or expressing feelings
- avoid feelings because they make me uncomfortable
- worry about my feelings making me fall apart
- be so concerned about hurting other people's feelings
- focus on food when I'm experiencing a painful emotion
- be hard on myself if I take a while to get the hang of this emotions thing
- dwell on my feelings after they've given me the information I need to make changes in my life

Imagine if you could succeed in doing everything on this *Do list* and avoid doing everything on this *Don't list*. You can!

☼ PRACTICE EXERCISE

Emotional Do & Don't List

PURPOSE: To recognize what steps you need to take in order to become emotionally healthy

RATIONALE: Creating personal *Emotional Do & Don't Lists* will push you toward ending unhealthy habits and developing healthy ones.

DIRECTIONS: Feel free to use the lists above as well as your rational beliefs for this exercise, but make sure your instructions are unique to you. First make a list of what you want to Do with your emotions, then make another for what you Don't want to do.

DO LIST

____

____

____

____

DON'T LIST

____

____

____

____

REFLECTION (to be done after completion of exercise): What is it like to see your intentions in black and white? Are you overwhelmed, exhilarated, or both? Are you scared that you can't live up to your list? If so, take a minute and remind yourself that the list is doable if you stay focused, remain patient, and keep practicing.

____

____

____

How do I go about actually experiencing my feelings?

If you want to experience feelings at the deepest level, you will need to "set the stage" correctly, which means maintaining an attitude of openness, acceptance, self-trust, curiosity, and self-compassion. Of course, you may be frightened that by allowing your emotions to flow, you'll never regain your composure and will run around weeping and wailing for the rest of your life. But, remember, *experiencing* your feelings is different from *expressing* them. Experiencing is an internal phenomenon, and expressing is an external one. Feeling angry and behaving angrily are like apples and oranges—two distinct (but clearly related) processes. When people say they're afraid of their feelings, what they usually mean is they're nervous about what they'll *do* if they allow themselves to get in touch with their discomfort. Make sure that you recognize the difference between the *process* of connecting to feelings and the *behavior* of expressing them.

If you've been hiding from or holding in emotions for a long time (or for a lifetime), initially, you may find yourself wearing them on your sleeve. Eventually, though, two things will happen. When you allow yourself to experience feelings on a regular basis—which is whenever they come 'round—they'll stop gushing like a geyser and start to ooze out more slowly. Also, as with any other endeavor, the more you interact with emotions, the better you'll get at bearing, expressing, and regulating them.

Like it or not, pain is an inevitable part of life.

To experience an emotion means just that—to be with it, immerse yourself in it, take it into your heart, let it bubble through or flow over you. The goal is to let the pain take root. Feeling pain is okay; it will pass. If you're someone who starts to experience a feeling, then panics and backs off when it grows intense, you'll need to buckle your seatbelt and hold on tight. There's no way around suffering. To paraphrase R.D. Laing, the brilliant British psychiatrist, *you either choose to feel whatever emotional pain comes along or to feel the pain that comes from choosing not to.* He is saying that, like it or not, pain is an inevitable part of life. The only real choice is between the original pain, or its consequence, the one that comes from avoiding it. Two kinds of pain, no escape: your choice.

Here are some tips to help you experience painful feelings:

- pay attention to your breathing and breathe normally, slowing your breath if it quickens or becomes shallow
- keep reminding yourself that you'll be fine
- remember that the feeling will pass
- focus on staying with the feeling and not pushing it away
- know that your pain has a purpose to ultimately enrich your life
- remind yourself that what you're feeling is normal
- know that no matter how intense, you can bear the pain just like everyone else
- tell yourself that nothing bad will happen, even if you feel your heart is breaking.

Believe me, nothing terrible will happen to you because you're suffering emotionally; the worst part is simply enduring the pain. By experiencing your feelings when they surface, they won't build to an intolerable intensity and become more difficult to bear later. Let them come in waves. There'll be moments of agony, which dissolve into a dull ache. In between flashes of acute emotion you may feel tired and depleted. Your muscles may tense, so try to relax and focus on breathing deeply and slowly. If you need to cry, cry. Sob, moan, wail, blubber, whimper, howl, keen, pound the pillow. *It doesn't matter what you do.* Trust that your body knows how to handle even the most excruciating feelings, that you can just let them happen, and that they'll eventually go away.

At some point, emotion will be spent and you'll probably be exhausted. That's all right. You just gave yourself an emotional workout. You've been in the vortex of your own personal tornado, so remain still, regain your internal equilibrium, and reenter the world slowly. When you're calmer, give yourself a pat on the back for having survived the bitterness of self-knowledge. Tell yourself that the next time you get scared of your emotions you'll remember that you made it through this time. Mark the occasion on a calendar or jot it down in a notebook. If you survived once, you can do it again—and again and again. Remind yourself that if you want to be mentally healthy, this is what you must do. Fortunately, as with any other practice, experiencing your feelings will become easier.

✓ STOP AND FEEL

How scared are you to experience your feelings?

____

____

____

What else can I do with feelings, other than experience them?

In addition to experiencing your feelings, you'll want to label them specifically and accurately so that you can recognize them again in the future. The next crucial step is to find out why you're feeling what you're feeling through a process called *reflection*—a combination of subjective and objective processing whose goal is to discover what suffering is trying to teach you. For example, you might think, *Okay, I felt completely helpless there for a while, utterly useless and powerless. What does that tell me about the situation that triggered the feeling? That there really is nothing to do but accept it? That I don't control the universe? That life means bearing losses? Or that I give up too easily and act as if I don't have options when I do?*

For example, maybe you're feeling ashamed about some terrible offense you think you committed. After sitting with your discomfort, take time to reflect on whether your offensive behavior was typical of you (and perhaps part of a larger pattern of not considering other people's feelings) or out of character. Was the shame yours or did it belong to someone else who projected it onto you? If you hadn't allowed yourself to feel the shame, would you have missed vital information about yourself or your situation?

> *The point is to use your discomfort to teach you how to make well-informed choices that will enhance your life.*

We talk of managing, controlling, dealing with, containing, handling, or coping with feelings, all of which are ways of trying to *regulate* emotions. This term means both to let your feelings go completely when they need free reign *and* to restrain them when losing yourself in them is not appropriate. This process requires use of your intellect, common sense, and sound judgment to determine what to do with emotions, all the way from experiencing to taking action based on them. Regulation is not choosing just one way to act with emotions or never varying your rigid stance. Rather, it is fluidly making decisions based on what and how much you're feeling and the context you are in.

For example, on a job interview, your prospects would be better served by sitting on, not delving into, your anger at the receptionist who forgot to tell the interviewer that you arrived an hour ago. Obviously, this is a time to control or contain your feelings, although you may return to thinking about the incident when the interview is over. Likewise, if you're having a case of pre-nuptial jitters, you need to shift into self-soothing mode to prevent yourself from calling the wedding off at the last minute. Recognizing that getting married is scary for everyone, letting your heart overrule your head would be unwise. However, if your daughter constantly talks back to you, you want the capacity to feel hurt as well as the verbal skills to express your disappointment. Without both, you might let her walk all over you. If you're diagnosed with a life-threatening illness, you need access to your emotions so that you can work through your fear, sadness, and helplessness. Finding ways to cope and people to support you will only come from getting in touch with what's going on inside you. As Kenny Rogers croons in one of his ballads, "You gotta know when to hold 'em and know when to fold 'em." That's what emotional regulation is all about.

When emotions are well regulated or managed, you experience and express them at an appropriate time and in an appropriate manner. When they're poorly regulated, you either bust a gut keeping them in, spill your guts without meaning to, or swing wildly from one extreme to the other. No one regulates their feelings perfectly, but those who've had more practice do better than those with less. The goal is to remain aware of feelings and work hard at figuring out how to handle them.

It's natural to feel pressure to *do* something with feelings, a byproduct of how uncomfortable suffering can be and society's focus on simplistic solutions. Sometimes tackling a problem head on is the right thing to do and absolutely necessary to improving your life. Other times, taking action precludes learning to accept life as it is. Just remember that action is fine as long as it grows organically out of experiencing and understanding what's going on inside you. If you don't allow the process to play itself out, your actions will be premature and arbitrary—which almost certainly will be detrimental to your long-term well-being. Here's what I mean: maybe you think you're angry, but when you dig deeper, you realize you're terribly hurt. Then when you hang out with hurt for a while, you discover that the name of this hurt is disappointment or betrayal. Responding from those feelings, or even hurt, is radically different from having an initial flash of anger and acting impulsively.

Sometimes, though, the best we can do is *cope* with our feelings. The word implies getting by, squeaking through, making do, and the truth is that sometimes this is all that's possible when you're in the throes of heated emotion. Hanging by your fingernails, teetering on the edge, about to get sucked under or bowled over—at times exerting all your power and will to keep it together is the best you can do. Sure, coping is better than not coping, but the ultimate goal is to gain the skills you need to become proficient at handling your feelings.

✓ STOP AND FEEL

Are you allowing yourself to sit with an emotion right now, or do you feel pressure to *do* something about or with it?

____

____

____

☼ PRACTICE EXERCISE

Controlling the Intensity of Affect

PURPOSE: To practice regulating the intensity of feelings

RATIONALE: This exercise will give you more practice regulating your feelings.

WHAT YOU NEED: a ball of thin string, scissors

DIRECTIONS: Cut the string into different lengths, from about 36 inches to 144 inches. Now tie each piece of string to itself to make a circle. You should have three to five circles when you're done.

Arrange them on the floor with the smallest on the inside and the largest on the outside so that you have larger and larger concentric circles. The smallest circle represents feelings at their most intense and the largest, feelings at their least intense.

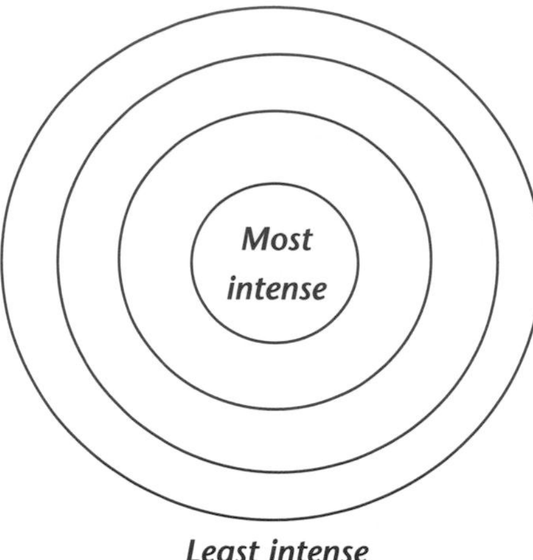

Stand inside the smallest circle and focus on a troubling emotion, one that's painfully acute. Now, as you step into the next circle, reduce the emotion by soothing yourself with calming self talk (and maybe a hug or two!). Continue reducing the intensity of affect as you move outward until you reach the outermost (least intense) circle. When the feeling has more or less dissipated, reverse direction and intensify the feeling as you make your way toward the center of the circle through anxious self talk. Repeat the exercise until you get the hang of regulating the force of your feelings.

REFLECTION (to be done after completion of exercise): Were you able to decrease or increase your affect? Was it harder to strengthen or weaken them? Don't worry if you have difficulty at first with regulation. Next time you're filled with intense affect, think about this exercise and mentally walk yourself through it to decrease your discomfort.

____

____

____

What are the barriers to experiencing feelings?

No matter how much you yearn to experience feelings, initially at least, you can expect a tug in the opposite direction, that is, to avoid intense affect. Remember, you've been doing emotional detours for a long time and feeling deeply may still be perceived as a threat to self. It will take a while for rational beliefs and healthy emotional practices to sink in and guide you toward feeling more freely.

In particular, a set of what Sigmund Freud called *emotional defense mechanisms* may get in the way. These are unconscious ways of thinking and/or behaving, which deny, falsify, or distort reality in order to protect you from emotional pain. Providing false comfort, however, they inhibit authentic feeling and the development of effective problem-solving. We all use them to greater or lesser extent when life gets too hot to handle. Problems arise when they kick in habitually and automatically or when they are so ingrained that we rigidly rely on them to feel okay about ourselves and our world.

Learning which defenses *you* employ and understanding how they hinder your emotional growth will help you stop using them. Although recognizing defenses is difficult because they generally function outside awareness, by familiarizing yourself with their descriptions and paying careful attention to how you react in situations, you'll begin to notice when they come rushing to your defense. The goal is to increase your awareness of your behavior and keep defensive practices at a minimum. Below are descriptions of some commonly-used defenses, adapted from the Diagnostic and Statistical Manual of Mental Disorders, Fourth Edition (known as the DSM-IV).

COMMONLY-USED DEFENSES

Acting Out

Taking action (usually impulsively and/or without regard to consequence) rather than employing reflection and effective problem-solving to reduce internal distress. Essentially, instead of experiencing emotion, you express it through unproductive or counterproductive behavior. Examples include binge-eating or overexercising, as well as any behavior which is done exclusively to discharge unwanted emotional tension and distract you from uncomfortable feelings.

Denial

Refusing to acknowledge an aspect of external reality or subjective experience that's apparent to others. When your savings account dips to below $100, and you blow $200 on concert tickets, you're denying external reality. When I ask a client entering my office near tears how she's feeling and she chirps, "Just fine," she's denying subjective experience. Denial is in play when you refuse to acknowledge that your low weight is unhealthy and dangerous or continue to believe that your next diet will fix your eating problems for good.

Devaluation

Putting down or thinking less of ourselves or others to avoid emotional discomfort. It's in motion when someone pays you a compliment about your gorgeous mocha brown eyes and you're so uncomfortable that you blurt out, "I hate them. They look like mud." Or when someone you admire hurts your feelings and you trash everything about them to make yourself feel better. You engage in devaluation when you don't think enough of yourself to get help for an eating disorder or when you put down people who do.

Displacement

Transferring (generally negative) feelings about a person onto a less-threatening substitute. You use displacement when you don't shed a tear over your mother's recent death, but bawl your eyes out when the lead character in a TV show dies of a similar disease. Or when you're furious at your boss, and come home and yell at the dog who did nothing but rush over to greet you warmly. It should come as no surprise that people with eating problems often displace their feelings onto food.

Help-rejecting Complaining

Repeatedly griping and asking for assistance, then rejecting the suggestions or advice you're given. This dynamic occurs because you're uncomfortable or have strongly mixed feelings about soliciting help. You might ask everyone you meet how to get out of your abusive relationship, but do nothing and act like a victim. You're being help-rejecting when friends suggest that you find a group to aid in overcoming your eating problems, and don't go but continue to complain about your weight.

Humor

Making light or joking about things that seriously concern you. You're using humor inappropriately when your mother says, "You look awfully thin," and you giggle and respond, "Moi? It must be your eyes that are shrinking." Or when you can't fit into clothes that are too tight, and make a flip remark about wanting to catch anorexia.

Intellectualization

Making generalizations and being theoretical to cover hurt feelings. When someone insults you and you go into a long, boring, detailed explanation about why you said what you said or try to defend it, you're distancing yourself from your hurt by answering from your head. After 9/11, if you put your entire focus on the politics of the situation and never connected to your fear, shock, and sadness, you were using intellectualization to avoid painful emotions. You use this defense when you respond to an upsetting comment about your weight by delivering a dissertation on the diverse history of beauty throughout the ages.

Minimizing

Making less of something to decrease emotional discomfort. You do this when you feel terrible about being betrayed by a friend, but tell her, "Oh, that's okay," or when your father beat you unmercifully and you inform your therapist that he only slapped you once or twice and that was because he was drunk. You're minimizing when you have a serious eating problem and insist you're just going through a phase, or when you pooh-pooh others' concerns about your unhealthy relationship with food.

Passive Aggression

Not expressing your negative feelings directly, but letting them be known in such a way that you can avoid taking responsibility for them. You're acting passive-aggressively when you're upset that your husband missed your birthday, tell him you don't mind, then "accidentally forget" to bring his pants home from the cleaners when you go to pick up your own. Or when your wife is trying to talk to you about a problem with the kids and you keep your headphones on but pretend you can hear every word she's saying. People around you may act passive-aggressively when they say they want you to be a healthy weight but subtly undermine your best efforts.

Projection

Disowning an unacceptable, uncomfortable thought, feeling, or behavior and attributing it to someone else. This happens when you can't bear to see the negative in yourself, but find it extremely distasteful in others. Projection is in action when a greedy person grouses about money-hungry people, when a pig-headed father accuses his son of being stubborn, or a when an overweight father ridicules his son for being fat. Projection is the way you toss the hot potato over to someone else. It's at work when you deny feeling badly about your eating problems and throw all your energy into helping your friend overcome her bulimia.

Rationalization

Finding a justifiable excuse, which puts a positive spin on a negative situation. You tell yourself that the reason you frequently get rejected is because no one's clever enough to see your potential, or insist that you eat, drink, gamble, or yell a lot because other people drive you to it. Telling yourself that you have to go on a binge or don't need to eat because you're upset is rationalizing—your attempt to magically transform bitterness into sweetness to make it palatable.

Repression

Unconsciously "forgetting" about something because it's too painful to take in or hold in awareness. Repression is unconsciously guiding your behavior when you keep missing and rescheduling a potentially painful dental appointment, when you can't recall being molested by your uncle though your sister insists it happened to both of you at his house by the lake on your eighth birthday, or when you have no recollection of smacking your child though you can see the red welt on his face. When you don't recall passing out from malnutrition because you eat so little, that's repression. Think of it as a trapdoor through which disappears an uncomfortable thought, feeling, or behavior.

✓ STOP AND FEEL

What are you feeling right now?

____

____

____

☼ PRACTICE EXERCISE

Defense Mechanisms

PURPOSE: To identify commonly-used defenses against feeling

RATIONALE: You'll only stop reacting unconsciously when you observe your behavior carefully and become aware of it. Identifying the defenses you use will help you recognize them in the future.

WHAT YOU NEED: list of defense mechanisms (just listed), pen

DIRECTIONS: Pick a defense mechanism you use frequently. Describe the situations that trigger it and what feelings it helps you avoid. Do this with as many defenses as you customarily use.

Defense Mechanism	*Triggering Situations*	*Protects Me From Feeling*

REFLECTION (to be done after completion of exercise): Was it difficult to identify your defense mechanisms? I expect it was, and that it may take quite a bit of self-examination for you to recognize them. Did you find that you use a variety of mechanisms or just a few? What do you need to do to stop using them?

____

____

____

Will my life improve when I start to feel my feelings?

I know that one of the ways you're psyching yourself up to "do right" by your emotions is by telling yourself that your life will improve when you do. It will—vastly, exponentially, and amazingly—but perhaps not right away. In fact, at first you may feel as if you've opened the floodgates and are drowning in a sea of heartache. Rest assured, feeling that you're at the mercy of your emotions will pass. When you stop denying or minimizing emotions or distracting yourself by focusing on food, you may even find that you're not fully yourself on the home or work front. That's okay and to be expected. Don't worry; you'll bounce back.

As you transform yourself now, remember a time when you made a successful major change in the past—quit your job to travel abroad, came out of the closet about your sexual preference, entered a grueling Ph.D. program, or began intensive weekly group therapy. Were you happy right away? Was there a stressful adjustment period when you were learning new things that were difficult? Did you have second thoughts that led you to want to give up? Was coping hard at the outset, then easier over time? Was the eventual gain worth the initial pain?

My guess is that you answered "Yes" to many of these questions and that, over time, you became more comfortable with your new situation and pushed your way through a rough transition to reach your goals. Growth is a process, and nowhere is this truer than in the realm of feelings. Building emotional muscle takes time and grit. So take a minute and adjust your expectations. Remember, pay-offs are at the *end* of the journey, not at the beginning. If you've made difficult major changes in your life and are now thriving as a result, look to that process and its successful outcome as a model for making strides in emotional management.

Don't be surprised by setbacks, regressions, and doubts that you're on the right track, and don't expect to reap rewards overnight. Refuse to give up merely because what you're doing is hard and scary, which, unfortunately, it will be. Don't look around at what other people are doing—or not doing—but keep your eyes on the prize. Set your sights on the twin goals of resolving your eating problems and using your feelings to improve your life. Before long, you'll see minor shifts, little green shoots that will give you hope that someday you'll have a whole, big, gorgeous, blooming, healthy garden. You might notice these positive changes yourself or hear about them from family, friends, or colleagues. Make sure not to let your small advances pass uncelebrated. They're like the first warm breath of spring.

Although you might feel strange connecting to feelings, almost as if you're inhabited by an alien being, the unfamiliarity will pass. You're getting acquainted with the new, upgraded version of you. Gradually, you'll have a sense of being more authentic, more centered and grounded, more connected to yourself. The greatest emotional shift may come as you move from secrecy or shame to experiencing greater pride your in thinking and your behavior. You may speak up or hold your tongue, find yourself making decisions differently than before, and acting in ways that surprise, delight, or shock you. Just take the changes as they come and have faith in the process.

You may even go overboard for a while as you move toward your heart's desires, prohibit others from taking advantage of you, say what you really think and feel, and make space and time for yourself. Or you might take baby steps that are tentative and feel your way cautiously and clumsily through the change process.

> *There's no right way to transform yourself. All you can do—all any of us can do—is be true to your emotions while using good judgment, and see what happens.*

Will becoming emotionally healthier change my relationship with other people?

When you start acknowledging and experiencing your emotions, *really* feeling them at the heart level, you may have a stronger urge to express them, especially if you've been holding them in for a long time. You may connect so strongly to certain emotions, like hurt, disappointment or loneliness, that you feel a need to say something to people who are causing you pain. Hopefully, a good number of them will appreciate your efforts and take your feedback to heart.

However, many people may like "the old you" better: meek and subservient, upbeat and non-complaining, or starving or stuffing away your feelings. Your attitudes, opinions, and behaviors may alarm, annoy, mystify, surprise, amaze, shock, enrage, or please other people. Beware—never, ever let anyone else's reactions deter you from experiencing your inner truth and expressing it appropriately. Sadly, those people may not have your best interest at heart.

Relationships may change as you reflect on your merits and frailties and decide that you're really not such a bad person, after all. You'll be less likely to hang around people who don't take you seriously, who disrespect your feelings, who project *their* shame onto *you* or try to manipulate your feelings, and who intentionally or unintentionally want you to buy into feeling worthless, incompetent, and a failure. These folks may be uncomfortable and angry when you take responsibility only for what you've done wrong and expect them to be accountable for their own mistakes and shortcomings. They may withdraw from you or redouble their efforts to keep the relationship as unhealthy as it was. A word of advice—if you know you're being honest with yourself and one of you has to be unhappy in the relationship, please, let it be the other person and not you!

It's crucial that you don't take other people's reactions to your feelings as an indication that you shouldn't feel or express them.

You have an inalienable right to your emotions, just as they have an inalienable right to theirs. Often, when you encounter a negative reaction to your feelings, it's not because you've done something wrong but because you've done something *right*—you've broken through your fear of hurting others and now they're uncomfortable or upset. Sometimes the fact that others are hurt by you means that you're getting seriously healthy!

Eventually, if you follow your emotions, you'll move away from people who don't make you happy and move toward people who do. Of course, there will always be some individuals in your life—most often family members—from whom you can't really escape. You'll learn to cope with them when need be, but populate the rest of your life with friends who think and feel like you do and who will help you find the best in your life for the rest of your life.

As I tell my clients and students, wait and see, and if you don't like who you are when you can handle your feelings better, you can always return to your old ways of emoting and relating. You can, but I guarantee you won't want to.

FURTHER EXPLORATION

1. What are three positive things you can say to yourself to make it easier to bear painful feelings?

___

___

___

2. What are the barriers to experiencing your full range of emotions, including fears and judgments, and especially secondary feelings?

___

___

___

3. What unconscious defense mechanisms do you use to avoid feeling deeply?

___

___

___

4. What beliefs do you need to change in order to lessen your use of these defense mechanisms?

___

___

___

5. What do you think are the pros and cons of experiencing painful feelings?

___

___

___

6. What are five ways your life will change for the better when you begin to experience your difficult feelings?

___

___

___

7. How will your transformation affect other people and your relationships? Who will be supportive? Who will be upset?

____

____

____

8. Into which part of the process—experiencing, reflecting on, or expressing emotions—will you have to put the most effort in order to grow and stop abusing food?

____

____

____

9. How strong is your commitment to feeling painful emotions—slight, weak, moderate, strong, passionate, unstoppable—and what could you do to strengthen it?

____

____

____

10. How might you get additional support connecting to your feelings (individual therapy, a self-esteem or assertiveness workshop, group therapy, writing a journal, using art, music, or dance)?

____

____

____

11. If you're afraid to join an eating and/or a support group to help you grow emotionally and deal with your food problems, what feelings and experiences are holding you back?

____

____

____

12. What indicators will show that you're making progress with your feelings?

____

____

____

13

Triggers to Intense Feelings and Disordered Eating

(Don't They Come With Safety Locks?)

If you love a good mystery, this chapter is for you! It will help you figure out why you shift into food mode when you're hit with tidal wave of emotion—and what to do about it. You know the behaviors: weighing yourself on the hour, doing a calorie count instead of your taxes, polishing off the desserts you planned to serve your dinner guests, or hanging out near your colleague's candy bowl when you're bored at work. If any of these mini-mysteries sounds familiar, it's time to don your Sherlock Holmes cap and discover what triggers you. A bit of sleuthing may be required, but once you've identified and collared the usual suspects, you stop yourself from getting robbed of your feelings in the future.

What is an emotional trigger?

Emotional triggers are external and internal stimuli that automatically activate a reaction within you, that is, they cause affective distress. Triggers may be people or events—a call from your elderly mother berating you for not visiting often enough or bumping into an ex-colleague who received the promotion you wanted. They also could be memories or thoughts about the future (called projections) that act like trip wires— recollections of the child you lost to cancer or angst about your upcoming salary review.

Think of your emotions as firecrackers: you're in no danger as long as they don't ignite (that is, get triggered). No matter how many firecrackers are stacked inside you, even dozens, you're safe as long as you don't strike a match. But the instant a flame lights one of your fuses, bam, instant Fourth of July.

When you find yourself triggered and are uncomfortable with your emotions, (which happens to all of us at times), you may act out in various ways, including the food arena, as a distraction from distress—planning your next diet, rushing off to exercise, or heading toward the refrigerator. This domino effect happens so fast that you might miss the trigger that set you off as well as your emotional response, and may only return to earth when you're exhausted from your workout or have finished off the last donut in the box.

HERE'S HOW THE TRIGGERING DYNAMIC WORKS:

(T) Trigger ⇨ (E) Emotion ⇨ (R) Food/weight-related Response

Example 1: External Trigger

(T) Call from mother ⇨ (E) Helplessness/Guilt ⇨ (R) Eat half a box of cereal

Example 2: Internal Trigger/Projection

(T) Thinking about work review ⇨ (E) Anxiety ⇨ (R) Readjust scale, take off clothes, and weigh self

Example 3: Internal Trigger/Memory

(T) Dead child's birthday ⇨ (E) Grief ⇨ (R) Calculate how much you've overeaten today and plan low-cal menu for tomorrow

Emotional triggers vary in intensity and visibility. Some are blatantly apparent, while others hover at the edge of awareness. Some set you off every time you encounter them, others press your buttons only when you're vulnerable and stressed. Some hit you head on, others sneak up from behind. It's impossible to live a full life without running into emotional triggers. Because you're not made of Teflon, the best you can do is to try to avoid the obvious ones, know what heats you up, and learn how to cool yourself down.

☼ PRACTICE EXERCISE

Emotional Triggers (Part One)

PURPOSE: To identify emotional triggers

RATIONALE: The more skilled you are at identifying triggers, the better your chance of not overreacting or of catching yourself before you do major damage.

DIRECTIONS: Using the following columns, recall the last time you acted out with food and write the emotional reaction you were trying to minimize or avoid. Backtracking, then identify whether an external event/person, an internal thought, or a memory activated your feelings. Keep generating triggers and repeating the process until you recognize common activators and what emotions they stir up.

Emotional Reaction	***External Trigger***	***Internal Trigger Anticipation***	***Internal Trigger Memory***

REFLECTION (to be done after completion of exercise): Are your triggers primarily internal or external? Are they memories or projections about the future? You may have a variety of emotional responses or only one or two. If you weren't able to identify at least a half dozen triggers, return to the exercise and keep going until you can.

____

____

____

☼ PRACTICE EXERCISE

Acting Out Emotions Through Food (Part Two)

PURPOSE: To identify what emotions provoke acting out around food and why

RATIONALE: After you've identified your triggers and the emotions they set off, you need to understand why you respond by acting out with food and which particular emotions drive you to it.

DIRECTIONS: Using the Emotional Reactions above, make a list of those that drive you to focusing on food. In the next column, write a food-related behavior you use to avoid or lessen emotional intensity—count fat grams, eat frozen Snickers bars, jump on the scale, do 100 sit-ups, stare at your naked body in the mirror, forage in food cabinets/refrigerator. In the last column, write your Rationale for keeping your distance from the emotion: *I feel overwhelmed, it makes me feel so alone, I'll get depressed, it hurts too much, I hate to cry, what's the point of dwelling on pain.*

For example your "Emotion" may be loneliness, your "Acting Out" could be trying on your skinniest clothes to cheer yourself up, and your "Rationale" may be that you're afraid you'll get depressed if you let yourself feel lonely.

Emotion	*Acting Out Behavior*	*Rationale*

REFLECTION (to be done after completion of exercise): Understanding what causes you to sidestep your emotions is vital, so make sure you think long and hard about your Rationales. Do you have just one or many? Are they rational or irrational? What can you do challenge the irrational ones?

____

____

____

What factors affect my ability to handle emotional triggers?

You now know that our basic motivation in life is to move toward pleasure and away from pain. Consequently, we're all generally drawn to and upset by similar circumstances. No one (at least if they're mentally healthy) enjoys being yelled at, getting physically hurt, failing, or losing a loved one. Most of us have visceral negative reactions to rejection, abandonment, grief, and humiliation. However, due to culture, biology, family, and individual experience, we also have a wide variety of expectations and tolerance for distress. Things that drive me crazy might not bother you, while something that has you climbing the walls might hardly ruffle my feathers.

Expectations

Your response to emotional triggers depends, to some extent, on what you expect in life. If you accept that life has up and downs and feel confident that you'll be able to weather rough seas, you won't be as roiled by upsetting circumstances as someone who believes that things magically should and must always work out for them. If you don't want to be ambushed by emotional triggers, you have to acknowledge that they're out there lying in wait. Recognizing that we all have roadblocks, detours, hills, and valleys on our life's journey will go a long way toward keeping your feet planted firmly on the ground and moving forward; sticking your head in the sand and pretending that life should be easy, fair, and just will nearly always leave you in shock and off balance when you hit a bump in the road.

Previous Experiences

The nature and extent of previous hurtful experiences also affects your ability to manage emotional triggers. If you've endured a lifetime of suffering, you may be extremely sensitive or you may (wrongly) believe you're so tough you can handle anything. If you were neglected, abused, or endured trauma as a child, each present day situation that is similar to your previous suffering may act as an emotional trigger, especially if your wounds haven't healed or if you're unaware of the damage they've caused. By coming to terms with your mistreatment or trauma, you'll learn what kinds of situations and interactions set you off, and then, either avoid them or put extra effort into dealing with them effectively.

General Circumstances

Naturally, your current circumstances are a partial predictor of how you'll react to triggers. If life is rolling along and your stress level is low to moderate, you may encounter one and be able to ignore or deactivate it fairly easily. You may even think, "Well, into every life a little rain must fall," and be on your merry way. However, if you're going through an ultra-stressful period and are already in over your head, a trigger may be the straw that breaks your emotional back.

Current Emotional State

Lastly, how you're feeling in the moment that you're triggered makes a big difference. If you're tense and jumpy, or feeling hopeless, you'll probably have a negative reaction. Something that's not normally a trigger might even escalate into one. However, if you encounter one when you're feeling especially upbeat, even if you're not all that pleased with life in general, it may barely register. Due to your current happiness, something that would normally spark a reaction might barely turn your head.

✓ STOP AND FEEL

What is emotionally triggering you right now?

____

____

____

☼ PRACTICE EXERCISE

Trigger Vulnerability Predictor

PURPOSE: To recognize factors that increase vulnerability to emotional triggering

RATIONALE: The better you are at recognizing what factors affect your vulnerability, the greater the chance that you can intervene and de-activate the trigger.

DIRECTIONS: Answer the following questions:

1) Are your expectations of life realistic or magical?

____

____

____

2) How do past trauma and/or mistreatment affect your inner world today?

____

____

____

3) In general, what is your satisfaction level with your life?

____

____

____

4) What's your usual temperament?

____

____

____

REFLECTION (to be done after completion of exercise): What factors make you vulnerable to triggers? What can you do to strengthen yourself in each area (for example, revamp your expectations to make them more realistic, take an anger management class, find a therapist to help with past trauma, make a major life change which will decrease stress)?

____

____

____

Can I overreact to triggers?

Sometimes you may overreact because of a feeling surge so powerful that it blows your circumstances out of proportion. Here are some over-the-top reactions: hearing about a party you weren't invited to and staying in bed all day, fuming for hours after a silly quarrel with the grocery clerk, or refusing to speak to your grandmother because she called a day late to wish you Happy Birthday. Although it feels authentic and justified in the moment, these responses are overblown. Rest assured, everyone overreacts this way once in a while.

Other times, however, when you *think* you're overacting, you actually may not be. If you were taught in childhood to stifle your feelings and to always keep a smile on your face and a song in your heart, displaying *any* negative emotion might feel excessive and scary when, in fact, your response is perfectly normal and natural. In this case, you're not overreacting at all, but have a misguided belief that experiencing or expressing strong emotions is wrong.

Three specific types of interactions, which are usually unconscious, often trigger intense emotions or overreactions. They are mental processes that occur deep in your psyche and are not readily apparent unless you're looking for them. To react appropriately when these dynamics occur, you need to become more conscious of when you're the initiator and recipient of them. Once you get the hang of spotting them—in yourself and in others—you'll have an easier time defusing them in an effective, appropriate manner. Moreover, these dynamics are exactly the ones that lead to such overpowering reactions that we feel we can't bear them and run off to abuse food instead.

Note that most of what's going on in these interactions is unconscious, out of your awareness, off camera. However, just because you can't recognize the dynamics doesn't mean they're not happening or affecting you. Let's take look at each one.

Active and Passive Projection

The first unconscious trigger of intense emotions is projection, of which there are two kinds—passive and active. *Passive projection* occurs when another person isn't aware of a feeling, that, if felt, would cause discomfort—and you pick up on it instead. *Active projection* happens when another person casts off an uncomfortable feeling, sends it your way, and you take hold of or internalize it as if it belonged to you. A useful metaphor to explain these complicated dynamics is that in passive projection someone drops a ball that you pick up; in active projection, someone throws it at you and you catch it.

There are two kinds of projection: passive and active.

Here's how passive projection works. Say you're on an airplane and notice a man leaving the lavatory and walking down the aisle clueless about the trail of toilet paper stuck to his shoe. If you're like me, your first reaction is to cringe. Why, you might ask, would *you* cringe when the toilet paper is on *his* loafer? Because you feel the shame you assume he'd feel if he knew the toilet paper was following him down the aisle (not that there's anything inherently shameful about having toilet paper on one's shoe!). In fact, the moment he looks down and notices the paper, you'll probably feel a wave of relief because he'll now feel the discomfort himself and remove it. In this case, since the man is a stranger, it's likely that your discomfort would be transitory and mild.

However, if it's your husband walking across a stage to make a presentation with toilet paper streaming off *his* shoe, my guess is you'd feel a good deal more shame, though it still doesn't belong to you. In fact, you might be similarly distressed if anyone close to you *behaves* shamefully. For example, if your brother has an addiction but is in denial or refuses to deal with it, you may feel ashamed for him when he does outlandish things. Unfortunately, *you're* experiencing the discomfort *he's* out of touch with and needs to feel in order to stop acting like a fool.

Although the discomfort feels enormously strong and as if it's your own, remember that the disgraceful actions of another person are not a cause for you to be ashamed. The feeling belongs to the individual acting badly. You need only feel shame about what *you* have done by your own free will. When you experience another person's discomfort because they don't or won't feel it, you need to let go of the feeling so that you're not carrying around someone else's baggage. We all have enough of our own to shlep through life.

Now let's take a look at *active projection*, which occurs when a person unconsciously disowns a feeling with which he or she is uncomfortable (or would be if it was felt) and lays it on you instead. As with passive projection, it's unlikely the person is aware that they're foisting their feelings onto you. The difference is that in active projection, the person is putting intention and effort (though unconscious) into avoiding emotional discomfort by sticking it on you, whereas in passive projection you're merely picking up on what they're ignoring.

To project is to *throw out* something, and in the case of active projection, the phrase has a dual meaning: both to divest the self of something and to thrust it as far away as possible. When someone actively projects a negative emotion onto you, it's because they're so uncomfortable with it (or would be if they allowed themselves to feel it) that they need to get rid of it post haste. They do this by attributing the uncomfortable feeling *to* you and then disliking or hating it *in* you, rather than in themselves. Think of the game of hot potato: When the potato is too hot to handle, it gets tossed to someone else. Remember, just because someone assigns a negative quality to you doesn't mean it is or isn't there; that's for you to decide.

An illustration of active projection is when your spouse has a thing about being right but denies it. In an argument, he or she insists, "You always have to have the last word. You always think you're right." If you can honestly look at yourself and say you're not someone who much cares about being right or wrong, then you have no reason to buy into the accusation. The zing of discomfort you feel belongs to your spouse who refuses to acknowledge hating to be wrong. How much easier to make *you* the fall guy for bad behavior!

The only healthy antidote to projection is to know yourself inside out. If you're completely objective and honest, you'll be able to distinguish your faults from what other people blame you for, and impartially evaluate their accusations.

Of course, if you always automatically assume that you're mistaken or wrong, it won't be easy to deflect projections. Remember, if the feeling doesn't belong to you, let it go.

Transference reaction

The second unconscious process that may get you going is called a *transference reaction*. It occurs when you're in a situation that's highly similar to one you've repeatedly experienced before, most often with your parents or other significant people in your childhood. Transference happens when, although you're well aware that you're in the present, your emotional system reacts as if you're in the past.

For instance, say your board chair calls and says she wants to talk about an upcoming meeting, but instead starts unloading her personal problems on you. After 15 minutes of complaining, you—or anyone—might start to feel uneasy. Now imagine that you had a mother who was emotionally immature, used poor judgment, and inappropriately confided in you as if you were her best friend. As a young child, of course you felt inadequate to take care of her or solve her problems. However, you also may have felt proud and honored that she turned to you in distress, as well as terrified that she'd fall apart or that you'd let her down. Now, in your current conversation with your board chair, you may re-experience the same feelings you had with your mother. Déjà vu…all over again.

Can you see the parallel? Instead of reacting as an adult and simply explaining that you have to get off the phone, you react as if you're a child and she's your mother. You may feel overwhelmed, enraged, invisible, incompetent, inadequate, paralyzed, or want desperately to fix her problems—whatever mix of emotions you felt with your mother when she expected you to listen (and maybe even solve) her problems. In essence, you're *transferring* the feelings you had (and still possibly have) about your mother onto the board chair.

Recognizing transference triggers is a huge asset to maintaining emotional equilibrium.

You're caught in a transference reaction when you're infuriated that your boss dismisses all your suggestions, just as you were as a child when your father systematically ignored your opinions. When you swallow your fury and clean up your irresponsible teenager's messes, the way you did for your siblings while your alcoholic mother lay passed out on the couch. When you fear making things worse by challenging your control-freak spouse because you got knocked around as a child every time you talked back to your parents. When you feel painfully left out because two friends mention going shopping together, which is exactly how you felt growing up when your twin sisters ran off hand in hand to do something without you.

To repeat, you're probably caught in a transference reaction when your response in the here and now is overblown or excessive to circumstance. The vulnerability and hurt you experience is not really about the present; it's about unhealed wounds from the past. This doesn't mean that you shouldn't have feelings about the current situation or person; it merely signals that the *intensity* of your reaction belongs to something that happened long ago.

The only way to counter a transference reaction is to closely observe when your feelings are out of proportion to a situation and reel yourself back from the past to the present. Remind yourself that you're an adult now with lots of emotional and cognitive options, that you don't have to stew in a rage or feel paralyzed, do someone else's bidding, or stand for being humiliated. You can speak up, walk away, or not take things personally, all of which you were unable to do growing up. Recognizing transference triggers is a huge asset to maintaining emotional equilibrium.

Beware of these common triggers: If you had a childhood full of neglect and felt invisible most of the time, when you feel unseen and unheard today, you're likely to react. If you were under constant scrutiny growing up, with minimal opportunity for self-sufficiency and autonomy, you'll probably have trouble being micromanaged today. You might also overreact if, as a child, you had excessive pressure to excel or behave perfectly, were severely restricted and/or harshly punished for minor infractions, witnessed abuse, or lived in a constant state of fear.

Repetition of the past

The third type of circumstance that can lead to an intense reaction is when you experience a *repetition* of painful situations or interactions that occurred in the past. For instance, if you've suffered a great deal of loss, again especially as a child, you may have an exceptionally rough time dealing with loss now. Remember, every loss contains reverberations of each previous loss. So for you to lose a sister to breast cancer at age 50 after losing your husband in your 40s and a best friend last year means your experience may be more charged than that of someone who has never had a soul close to them die.

There's really no way around this kind of cumulative reaction, no matter how strong it is, other than acknowledging it. If you've endured a lot, you're carrying with you all your grievances and wounds of the past, and each new hurt will remind you of old ones. You feel what you feel and that's that. The most important thing is not to judge yourself for having a more intense reaction than someone else. If they had lived your life, they might respond exactly the same way.

✓ STOP AND FEEL

What are you feeling right now?

____

____

____

☼ PRACTICE EXERCISE

Rescripting

PURPOSE: To develop effective ways of reacting to triggers

RATIONALE: It's hard to change your behavior without understanding its causes and underlying dynamics. By becoming conscious of what's going on, you can make your responses more appropriate.

DIRECTIONS: Think of a troubling situation that involves a transference reaction, repetition of previous wounding or trauma, or internalizing someone's negative projections. Play out the scene in your head, including your usual reaction. Then replay the scene with a different ending (or reaction). For example, if you usually remain silent when your boss criticizes you just like your father did—a transference reaction—imagine speaking up. Or if you generally respond with vitriol and sarcasm, picture yourself saying nothing and walking away.

CURRENT SITUATION (TRANSFERENCE REACTION, REPETITION OF PAST, OR NEGATIVE PROJECTION)

USUAL REACTION

NEW REACTION

REFLECTION (to be done after completion of exercise): Were you able to put a different spin on each triggering scenario? What got in the way of changing your behavior? If you want to avoid getting triggered, practice rescripting every troubling circumstance, either beforehand to interact differently, or afterward, to determine how to do better next time.

How can I stop acting out with food in response to emotional triggers?

Triggers will continue to lead to knee-jerk, destructive impulses around food unless you tackle the problem from multiple angles and make different decisions at specific choice points. You will need to stay focused on three areas simultaneously to achieve success: changing your beliefs about triggers, food, and emotions; learning how to identify and handle your feelings effectively; and eliminating acting out with food by developing new self-care strategies.

Let's run through your options using an example of an external, ongoing trigger to see what you can do to change the outcome of a situation. Say that every week you spend time with Uncle

Charlie who's more than a bit of a grouch now, but who was a favorite of yours in childhood. You feel badly for him, yet come away from each visit vowing it will be your last and fuming with hostility—resentment that he's eating up your precious leisure hours, anger that all he does is complain, disappointment that he rarely expresses any interest in your life, and helplessness that you can't get out of what you feel is your duty. It never fails, you're barely out the door of Charlie's nursing home room and you're obsessing about food.

Changing Your Beliefs

The first thing you could do to change the outcome of your visit is to alter your thoughts about Charlie and your duty toward him so that you won't feel so triggered. Rather than feeling guilty about considering skipping a weekly visit, you could decide that seeing him every other week is perfectly acceptable and fair. Or you could stop thinking of him as a burden, and remind yourself of all the kind things he did for you when you were a child. You could focus your thoughts on how good the visits are for him, not on how bad they are for you, or markedly reduce what you expect of him. All these are ways of changing your beliefs, which then alters your feelings, and ultimately, impacts your need to act out with food.

You might also want to reframe your beliefs about how you expect to react. If you tell your sister, "Every time I visit Uncle Charlie, I'm disappointed," you're programming yourself for—guess what—being let down. Change your beliefs about your emotions, and you'll actually feel differently. Tell yourself that when you leave him you'll feel proud, calm, compassionate, or even that you won't feel much of anything. By deciding what you want to feel about the visit, you can gently push away other unwanted feelings.

Finally, you can address the beliefs that underlie acting out with food. Again, if as you're saying goodbye to Charlie you think, "I have to have that piece of chocolate cake" or "I'm so fat, I'd better throw out those cashews or I'll eat them all," you're setting yourself on a path of destruction. Even if you're upset when you arrive home, you can have a set of beliefs that says you don't need to focus on food because you can take care of yourself just fine without it. Think: *What if there was no such thing in the world as food—what would I do then?* Make sure that the tape running in your head is healthy, and your behaviors will follow.

PRACTICE EXERCISE

Reframing Triggering Beliefs

PURPOSE: To reframe beliefs in order to decrease triggering

RATIONALE: When you think differently, you can't help but feel and act differently.

DIRECTIONS: Choose a situation or person that triggers distressing feelings and destructive eating. Below, list your current beliefs about a situation that triggers you to act out with food. For example, Uncle Charlie beliefs might include: *Seeing him is a drag, I have better things to do with my time, I'm bummed he doesn't care about me, I can't help but leave there mad, I'm too upset when I get home to do anything fun, hanging out with him makes me just want to hurt myself. If I focus on food I'll calm down.* Then reframe all the irrational beliefs about your situation to make them rational.

Situation ____

____

____

Irrational belief	**Reframed rational belief**
____________________	____________________
____________________	____________________
____________________	____________________
____________________	____________________

REFLECTION (to be done after completion of exercise): Was it harder to identify or reframe your irrational beliefs? Which new rational beliefs will give you the most pay-off—Triggers, Emotions, or Responses? If you act out of these beliefs in the future, how will that change your life?

____

____

____

Handling Feelings

Along with creating healthier beliefs, you can also work on handling your emotions differently. Returning to Uncle Charlie, you would first have to get under your initial responses of anger and resentment to understand the complexity of your reactions. Maybe you're frustrated and disappointed that he doesn't take any interest in you, but know how much your visits mean to him. Deep down you feel hurt and unappreciated and that's causing your anger. If you didn't believe that Charlie should be grateful for your time with him, you would visit him because you believe it's the right thing to do and leave feeling neutral or happy to have been of service! Often, once you get to the root of your feelings, they not only relieve you of the need to act out with food, but help you understand yourself (and other people) better.

When negative feelings about Charlie surface, you can remind yourself that they're only temporary and will pass or feel proud of doing more for your uncle than other family members do. You can laugh inwardly at his caricature-of-a-curmudgeon behavior, be curious about how he became so grumpy, or have compassion for someone who is so obviously bitter and unhappy. By changing your view of Charlie and your situation, you can't help but generate different, less-discomfiting feelings.

☼ PRACTICE EXERCISE

Regulating Emotional Reactions

PURPOSE: To regulate your emotional response to triggers

RATIONALE: You can regulate your emotions by focusing attention on them to either increase or decrease their intensity.

DIRECTIONS: Using the Trigger situation or person you chose for the Beliefs Exercise, identify the painful emotions that generally cause you to act out with food. (Uncle Charlie examples include: resentment, hurt, frustration, disappointment, and feeling undervalued.) Next, consider what you need to do with your feelings—connect more deeply because you generally push them away or soothe them because you know all too well how painful they can be—to really take care of yourself. (Uncle Charlie examples include: pull out photos of you and Charlie long ago having fun and have a good cry, call your sister and complain, write your heart out in your journal, put your hand over your heart and send healing messages to yourself, ask your partner or a friend for a big hug). Make sure to identify all your emotions of the situation.

Situation/person ______________________________

____

Emotion #1 ______________________________

New regulation strategies ______________________________

____

____

____

Emotion #2 ______________________________

New regulation strategies ______________________________

____

____

____

Emotion #3 ______________________________

New regulation strategies ______________________________

____

____

____

REFLECTION (to be done after completion of exercise): Were you able to identify the emotions that trigger a food response? How did you do with either increasing or decreasing your affective reaction? How will your new regulation strategies help you with disordered eating?

____

____

____

Eliminating Acting Out With Food

Even when you're unable to change your beliefs or handle your feelings effectively, you still have a third intervention point to prevent you from acting out through dysfunctional eating. The key is to make a decision that *no matter what emotion you're experiencing, you refuse to use or abuse food to feel better*. Any healthy behavior is fair game; the point is to choose to do something other than taking your feelings out on your appetite and your body.

Although the ultimate goal is to experience all your feelings, initially you may not be able to do that. If you can sit with how disappointed you are at Uncle Charlie or how much you miss his former self, fine. If not, you need to distance yourself from your emotions so that they don't overpower you and prompt you to do something unhealthy to your body and spirit. Possibly you don't have the skills yet to contain your feelings, and have to distract yourself instead. Okay, then, find some activity—any behavior that isn't self-destructive—to refocus you and buffer your emotions.

PRACTICE EXERCISE

Stopping Acting Out With Food

PURPOSE: To avoid acting out with food in spite of an intense emotional reaction

RATIONALE: You can train yourself not to abuse food by engaging in other (distracting) activities, even when you're emotionally upset.

DIRECTIONS: Continuing with your Trigger situation, brainstorm the specific behaviors you can do to distract yourself from your feelings and refocus your energies. (Uncle Charlie examples include: call a friend, take a nap, go for a walk, do some chores, listen to a relaxing CD, or browse on the computer.).

Situation/person ____

____

Distraction activities

____

____

____

REFLECTION (to be done after completion of exercise): Could you think of enough distractions? What got in the way of brainstorming activities? What would prevent you from following through with your distractions?

____

____

____

Lastly, even if you're unable to intervene in any of these ways and end up using or obsessing about food to make yourself feel better, you can *always* reflect on your behavior afterward with compassion and curiosity to learn from it. Chances are that next time you'll be able to make better choices, and if not then, the time after that. It doesn't matter at which point you intercede; the point is to break the pattern and do *something* differently.

What else can I do to separate food and feeling?

Scrutinizing your thoughts, feelings, and behaviors is tough work, but it's the only way to get from here to there. Because this is a book about food and feelings, you will need to work both ends of the process to reach your goal of using each appropriately. This means doing whatever is necessary to put each in good working order. Remember that the more successful you are in identifying and handling your emotions, the easier it will be to avoid acting out with food. Alternately, the more effective you are in disengaging from unhealthy eating, the more chance your emotions will have to blossom and guide you toward authentic happiness.

You've probably figured out by now that transforming your emotional world means trying on lots of new behaviors. If you careen wildly through life, zooming from one crisis to another without stopping to examine what you feel, you'll have to slow down, digging deep in order to connect to your inner world, understand what your emotions mean to your life, and consider how they impact your relationship with food. Why not spend a few minutes at the end of each day recalling what emotions you experienced or writing them down in a journal? This activity is an excellent substitute for a day's end calorie count, a self-trashing for overeating, or a midnight snack.

Conversely, if you believe that every waking moment must be brimming with passion or heartache, you'll need to learn how to modulate emotions so that they don't overpower and rule you. Intense emotions can certainly make you feel alive, but they need to be complemented with good judgment and clear thinking. Your work is to get your head in gear, and give your heart a rest! Once you're in better balance, it will be easier to curtail food-related behaviors that hurt you and expand self-care activities that heal you.

Lastly, if you're generally angry, anxious, or defensive—basically an unhappy person—you're setting yourself up to fail at breaking the food-feelings bond. It's one thing to have moments of upset and angst and quite another to suffer from chronic dissatisfaction or melancholy. All someone needs to do is scratch your emotional surface, and you're bound to fly off the handle or plunge into despair. Until you realize that your view of the world acts like a magnet to emotional pain, you'll continue to suffer. Moreover, your negative reactions are bound to be so intense that they overshadow your best intentions to change your relationship with food.

Many chronic emotional states or conditions make it difficult to be a happy, productive member of society—as well as prevent you from functional eating. Perhaps you're depressed, suffer from an anxiety disorder, or haven't healed from long ago or recent trauma. *Unless you deal with what's causing emotional blockages and ruptures, you won't be able to heal your pain or maintain healthy eating habits.* What keeps you from exploring the roots of your unhappiness? What prevents you from getting the help you need to become the person you want (and deserve) to be?

If you can't figure out why you're a walking time bomb, a well of loneliness, or a hive of anxiety, you can read self-help books on emotional health and trauma, keep a journal of your emotions to help you track and understand them, share your feelings with understanding, compassionate friends, or take a workshop on how to be more assertive or how to relax with yoga. Last, but not least, if you've done all of the above and are still unable to change, you can seek out professional help.

✓ STOP AND FEEL

What feelings stop you from getting the help you need to improve your life and repair your relationship with food?

____

____

____

Most of the strategies I've given you for handling emotions and eating more sanely focus on making internal adjustments, but another avenue for transformation also exists: rather than change yourself, you can change your environment. Allowing yourself to remain in chronically stressful situations is nothing less than unhealthy and will make it nearly impossible to end your self-destructive reactions to food and weight. If you're sick and tired of going out to lunch with friends who constantly talk about dieting and losing weight or who complain and are going nowhere in life, it's time to find some new buddies. If every time you visit your son and daughter-in-law, they expect you to join them in cleaning the house, you'll need to find another venue for getting together. If work is stressing you out because you're doing the job of two people and your boss refuses to hire additional help, maybe you need to find work that's doable and brings you pleasure. If you're miserable in an abusive relationship, read the writing on the wall, gather your courage, get some help, and walk away.

Recognizing your emotional and eating triggers—and changing your responses—is challenging work. Triggers, however, are nothing more than buttons that get pushed when you think you can't help yourself. Maybe you've been telling yourself you can't for a long, long time, or maybe you've wanted to change, but don't know how. Keep focused on all three tracks—transforming unhealthy beliefs, coming to terms with your feelings, and monitoring your behavior around food. Your triggers will gradually move from the forefront to the background of your life. Not only that, you'll increase your confidence and self-trust and start to experience the pure joy that comes from making peace with food and taking care of yourself with consideration and compassion.

FURTHER EXPLORATION

1. Are you easily triggered to anger, fear, hurt, or disappointment?

2. What are your major triggers (people and situations)?

3. What are the most difficult emotions for you to bear (anger, anxiety, self-doubt, disappointment, helplessness), and why?

4. How can you alter your circumstances (that is, your environment) to be triggered less often and/or less intensely?

5. What relationships do you need to change to be triggered less often?

6. What are your expectations about being able to defuse triggers and prevent acting out with food?

7. Are there any unhealthy behaviors besides eating that you're worried you'll engage in if you no longer abuse food?

8. What is the biggest obstacle for you to overcome so that you won't be triggered to act out with food?

14

Feeling Your Way to Happiness, Health, and a Natural Body Weight

(Sold—I'll Take All Three!)

Much of this workbook has been about what to do with the painful feelings that make us unhappy. Now it's time to take a look at the other end of the emotional spectrum—how you can experience the happiness you so richly deserve. Beware—being happy is not the same as *not* being unhappy. Nor is happiness a perpetual state of being: it comes and goes. Finding it takes focus, effort, good judgment, persistence, and the ability to fine-tune life choices. The more you know about what makes *you* truly happy, the better you will be at finding it. Pleasure, joy, contentment, and satisfaction may be sitting on your doorstep, but they're not going to reach up and ring your bell!

To some people happiness equals excitement, status, and "the good life," while to others it's a sense of inner peace, small satisfactions, and everyday delights. Sadly, we too often allow cultural messages or other people (well-meaning parents, teachers, or peers) to determine what will make us happy. We're so bombarded with messages that we may never have stopped to think about what really rings our chimes. Or we race from moment to moment, seeking pleasure like bees searching for nectar, without pausing to take a step back and look at the big picture. In order to make the best use of emotions, you have to take in the forest as well as the trees. Creating happiness in this troubled world requires considerable soul searching and an ongoing commitment to emotional health. You need to stay tuned to your "feelings channel," reflect on your emotional and behavioral patterns, understand how you fit into the world, and know what you want out of your brief time on earth.

In order to lead an enjoyable, satisfying life, you have to start with beliefs that support your right to happiness. If you believe you're condemned to an existence of dreariness or suffering and don't deserve authentic happiness, it will forever be out of reach. If joy and contentment generate secondary emotions of guilt about feeling "too good" or of fear that the other shoe will drop and pleasure will vanish, happiness will continue to elude you. The only way to be sure you're bound for happiness is to have rational beliefs that encourage and applaud its pursuit.

BELIEFS ABOUT HAPPINESS

IB: Happiness never lasts.
RB: Happiness doesn't stay, but it always returns.

IB: It's sinful to want to be happy.
RB: There's nothing sinful about wanting to be happy.

IB: I'll be happy when I'm thin.
RB: I can be happy at any weight.
RB: Being thin won't necessarily make me happy.

IB: It's shallow to focus on being happy.
RB: It's normal to focus on being happy.

IB: I don't deserve to be happy.
RB: Everyone deserves to be happy.

IB: I'm destined to be unhappy for the rest of my life.
RB: No one is destined for happiness or unhappiness.

IB: There's no point in being happy because the feeling always ends.
RB: The point of being happy is in experiencing it.

IB: I shouldn't have to work to find happiness.
RB: I need to apply myself to achieve happiness.

IB: I have no right to want happiness.
RB: The pursuit of happiness is an inalienable right.

IB: Only food makes me happy.
RB: Many things make me happy.

IB: Nothing makes me happy.
RB: I have to learn what makes me happy.

IB: My being happy will cause other people to be unhappy.
RB: Other people will survive being unhappy.
RB: I need to create my own happiness and others need to create theirs.

☼ *PRACTICE EXERCISE*

Beliefs About Happiness

PURPOSE: To identify your rational and irrational beliefs about happiness

RATIONALE: You won't find happiness unless you have a belief system that encourages it. Conversely, if you believe you deserve to be unhappy, that's how you'll end up.

DIRECTIONS: Below, write your beliefs about happiness by using the ones just listed and/or creating your own. Focus on the verbal and nonverbal messages about being happy that you received growing up and check to see if they hold true for you today. Don't worry whether your beliefs are rational or not. Pay special attention to ones that lead to negative secondary emotions about happiness such as feeling ashamed when you're happy or fearing it won't last. When you're done, reframe irrational beliefs into rational ones.

Beliefs about Happiness

____

____

____

Reframed Irrational Beliefs about Happiness

____

____

____

REFLECTION (to be done after completion of exercise): What is it like to examine happiness? Were most of your initial beliefs rational or irrational? How do irrational beliefs hinder achieving authentic happiness?

____

____

____

Once you have sound, functional beliefs about happiness, you can move on to using emotions at specific choice points to lead you away from pain and toward pleasure. Here's an example. Say you're single with a well-paying, satisfying job, own a condo, are in glowing health, and have a host of friends and acquaintances. After a slew of failed relationships, you gave up dating, but are now ready to seek out a permanent partner. Through a dating service, you come up with three reasonable prospects and arrange to meet them. After Date #1, you arrive home astounded that your date never asked one question about you, flirted with the wait staff, and was rude when you begged off early. Mildly disappointed, you remain hopeful that one of the other two prospects will pan out.

Date #2 was sweet, intelligent, easy to be with, attractive but no movie star. You were surprised at how many things you had to talk about, but felt zilch in the chemistry department. Without caring much, you've agreed to get together next week. You floated home after Date #3 who oozed sex appeal and self-confidence, entertained you with amusing anecdotes, and showered you with compliments. You were gaga from the moment you met and in a fog the rest of the evening. After a few hot and heavy goodnight kisses, you exchanged phone numbers and talked about where you'd go on your next evening together.

Let's stop and review your emotions. You felt invisible and devalued by Date #1 and are clear that you don't want to get together again. You have mixed feelings about Date #2. Although there were enjoyable moments, you're appropriately concerned about the lack of physical attraction, and are left feeling ambivalent—neither turned off nor turned on. In contrast, Date #3 really got your juices flowing. Overpowered by attraction, you're having a hard time focusing on any other qualities.

You go out with Date #2 again, have another pleasant evening, and discover more common interests. This time you get a better-than-expected parting kiss, and return home feeling relaxed and satisfied by time well spent. When Date #3 didn't call, you left a voice mail message, received an encouraging one back three days later, returned the call, but have heard nothing more.

Once again, let's stop and examine what you might be feeling. You remain ambivalent about Date #2, but see some potential there. You're still hot to trot based on Date #3's upbeat phone message, but also feel let down and a little annoyed. Plus you have that old nagging feeling in the pit of your stomach—what you used to call excitement, but now recognize as anxiety. You decide to give Date #3 another call, and if there's no rapid return of interest, to chalk it up.

Now it's time to assess whether your emotions are doing their job, that is, moving you toward ultimate pleasure and away from ultimate harm. Although Date #2 may not be "the one," you're not picking up any danger signals either. Having nothing to lose and everything to gain, you determine that continuing to see Date #2 is good for you. However, since those old familiar butterflies point toward eventual heartbreak, you decide that Date #3 is not good for you and don't plan on pursuing a relationship.

I could run step-by-step through dozens of scenarios to illustrate how emotions are your perfect guides to happiness. Of course, life is messy and unpredictable, and following your feelings won't guarantee eternal bliss. However, if you fail to pay attention to your emotions, how will you ever get what you want and deserve? Once you get the hang of valuing *all* your feelings, you'll wonder how you ever managed without them. And you'll have one more reason not to abuse food when your heart is sending you a message.

✓ STOP AND FEEL

Now that you're nearing the end of this book, how are you feeling about overcoming your eating problems and becoming emotionally healthy?

____

____

____

☼ PRACTICE EXERCISE

What Makes You Happy?

PURPOSE: To identify what specific activities bring you happiness

RATIONALE: It's important to plan for happiness and not to expect it to just happen. You need to know specifically what makes you happy and the steps you need to take to achieve it.

WHAT YOU NEED: imagination and focus, pen

DIRECTIONS: In each of the four self-care realms below, list one goal that will increase your happiness. Under Physical you might write, *to eat "normally"* or *to learn how to relax*; under Mental, *to be more challenged at work*, under Emotional, *to not take things so personally* or *to become more assertive*, and under Spiritual, *to spend more time alone in nature*. When you're done with your goals, return to each one and write down one step to help you reach them. For wanting to be more challenged at work, you could write, *review job description* or *talk with boss about new projects.*. For wanting to become more assertive, *read a book on saying No without guilt* or *attend an assertiveness workshop*.

Emotional

Goal ____

Step ____

Physical

Goal ____

Step ____

Mental

Goal ____

Step ____

Spiritual

Goal ____

Step ____

REFLECTION (to be done after completion of exercise): Was it hard to come up with goals for each part of your life? Which was easier, identifying goals or the steps to reach them? Were there realms for which you couldn't come up with a goal? Is that because you're already happy or because you're stumped?

____

____

____

Will experiencing my feelings really change my relationship with food?

When you begin to use your feelings as a guide, you'll notice a shift in your attitude towards food and eating. You may take a greater or lesser interest in food, eat at home more often or eagerly check out every restaurant in town, find you enjoy cooking elaborate meals or decide you have better things to do with your time, become more curious about Recommended Daily Allowances or loosen up and break an occasional nutrition rule. If you're a compulsive eater, you may come home after a hellish day at work ready to hit the Haagen Dazs and suddenly realize that it's lost its appeal. As a restrictive eater, you might intentionally pass by your favorite bakery dreaming about having a croissant, only to circle back and go for it.

Many clients get angry at this point in their recovery, and more than a few have come charging into a therapy session accusing me of ruining their lives. In a bind, they feel stuck and scared because food (eating it or not eating it) has stopped being the panacea it once was. Other clients express sadness that in order to become healthy and live a better life they have to say goodbye to their food obsession, a faithful old buddy. If you feel this kind of loss, don't worry. You *will* get to the other side. When you repeatedly recognize that a preoccupation with food and weight doesn't *really* take care of you emotionally, you'll mourn for a while, and when you're done, you'll go looking for what is truly fulfilling.

One of the best parts of experiencing your emotions—aside from gaining self-knowledge—is the incredible pride that comes from not abusing food. You might even discover that this achievement gives you confidence to change other things that aren't working in your life. In truth, your eating struggles may have been your way of avoiding issues that really do require attention. Now that you've gained inner strength and resources, they may not be so overwhelming, depressing, or frightening to tackle. By listening to your heart *and* possessing the confidence born of succeeding at a major personal revolution, you'll gain the skills you need to address any problem.

A word of caution. It's quite possible that when emotions become especially difficult and intense, you'll occasionally revert to old habits. If so, be compassionate and curious—not judgmental—about your behavior. Give yourself a break for being human, and focus on the successes and strides you've made eating in a healthy, nurturing way. Remind yourself that you have better choices than eating or depriving yourself of food and refocus on the activities you've been using to effectively take care of yourself.

✓ STOP AND FEEL

What are you feeling right now?

___

___

___

☼ PRACTICE EXERCISE

Food and Feelings

PURPOSE: To help you discover your feelings about individual foods

RATIONALE: If you want to make satisfying eating choices, you have to know what you feel—from disgust through neutrality to ecstasy—about everything on your plate.

WHAT YOU NEED: Table, chair, foods

DIRECTIONS: Gather together three foods, one from each category: 1) a food you dislike because of its taste, consistency, or negative associations, 2) a food whose taste you crave and adore, 3) a food you can take or leave. Put each food on a different plate. Take a taste of one (it doesn't matter which), eat very slowly, and notice how you feel about this food—neutral, repelled, disgusted, or crazy about it. Mixing up the order, perform another round of tasting and continue until you've connected to your feelings about each food.

REFLECTION (to be done after completion of exercise): What did you notice about your reactions? Were your responses both physical and emotional? Did you react differently than you expected because you ate slowly?

___

___

___

How will I know my body's natural weight?

If you're serious about discovering your natural weight, you'll have to accept the fact that your body knows better than your mind the weight at which it is most comfortable and healthy. This means that you can't pick a number based on a magazine article, weight chart, or what your friends, parents, spouse, or even your doctor tell you. You can't return your body to the weight or shape it was in high school and you can't mold it into "celebrity perfect" by starving yourself or overdoing it on the track or at the gym. But by taking this book to heart, getting to know your inner world, and straightening out your relationship with food, there's an excellent chance that your body will arrive at a weight that's right for you.

☼ PRACTICE EXERCISE

Reframing Beliefs about Your Shape

PURPOSE: To create a belief system that supports loving and accepting your body at any size

RATIONALE: You may not realize how much your beliefs influence how you feel about your body and everyone else's. Society and family messages are internalized so subtly and early in life that we sometimes forget *they're not Truth.*

DIRECTIONS: Write down all your beliefs about weight, body shape and size. Try not to sanitize your list if you run into ones that shock or upset you. Keep going until you have enough beliefs to give you a sense of your values about your body. Now sift through them and reframe all those that aren't rational. When you're done, you'll have a belief system that fosters body acceptance.

Weight/Shape/Size Irrational Beliefs	**Weight/Shape/Size Reframed Beliefs**
______________________	______________________
______________________	______________________
______________________	______________________
______________________	______________________

REFLECTION (to be done after completion of exercise): What was it like to think about underlying body beliefs? Was it hard to separate what you think from what you believe is The Truth? (I bet it was!) How can you maintain a healthy belief system about your body? What else can you do to eliminate or reduce body shame?

____

____

____

Weight is the final topic to talk about in this workbook for a reason—it's the end product of connecting with feelings and making peace with food. Even if you don't reach what you consider your "ideal" weight, by restructuring your beliefs and experiencing your emotions, you'll be moving toward a more satisfying, gratifying life. Real happiness comes from inside; it cannot be lost or gained by what you eat or by moving a pound or two (or ten) in either direction. Trust me, once you're experiencing all your feelings on a regular basis and leading a fulfilling life, a number on the scale or a clothing size will begin to mean less and less to you.

In fact, rather than thinking about weight, why not put your energy into getting fit and healthy? If you insist on focusing on numbers, start with these: your blood pressure, cholesterol, triglycerides, bone density score, pulse, and resting heart rate—numbers that will make a *real* difference in your life. Need some more to mull over? How about your sodium intake, how many glasses of water you drink a day, the number of servings of fruit, vegetables, and whole grains you eat in a week, your calcium and vitamin D intake, and the right balance of nutrients for your age, gender, and lifestyle.

Clients frequently ask if they should concentrate on eating nutritiously above all else. My answer is always the same: once you've found a comfortable weight that you can maintain by "normal" eating, then, *and only then*, is it time to tweak your diet to include more nutritious foods. Focusing on "eating healthy" early in the transformation process can too easily push you back into the diet mentality of "good" and "bad" foods and cause you to feel deprived and disconnected from your body. After you're truly comfortable around food, you can begin to modify your eating to make it more wholesome and healthful—eating more whole grain products, fruits, and vegetables, cutting out transfats as much as possible, avoiding processed foods, even finding products that are tasty *and* low in sugar and salt. Sometimes you'll be satisfied with "healthier" versions of your favorite foods and sometimes you won't. You'll just have to experiment.

However, be careful not to replace your pre-occupation with food and weight with an obsession about nutrition. By all means, feed your body high quality, natural, nutrient-filled foods, but please enjoy what you're eating! Better to have half a donut which tastes divine than a slab of no-fat, sugar-free pound cake that could easily be mistaken for cardboard. Remember "normal" eaters don't eat only from nutritious food groups. Eating healthy foods is an absolute must for physical self-care, but it's important to keep nutrition and sensory pleasure in balance.

> *Finding a natural body weight is a process, just like working with your feelings and learning to eat "normally."*

Right now you might be at the beginning or in the middle of this endeavor. By the end, you'll discover the body weight that is most comfortable and healthy for you. And by weight, I don't mean one single number. Most of us fluctuate several pounds one way or the other from one day or week to the next. The range will also likely vary over your lifetime, so what was healthy for you ten years ago may be a little more or less today. By giving yourself leeway, you won't obsess about what the scale says; instead you'll be paying attention to what you're eating and feeling.

Hopefully, some day, you'll ditch your scale and stop worrying about what you weigh once and for all. Metabolic and hormonal problems aside, if you're eating in a balanced way, and getting moderate exercise, your weight *will* stabilize at what's healthy for you over time. It might be higher than you wish and you might have a different shape or size than you hoped, but it will be the *weight that's relatively effortless for you to maintain when your appetite and activity level are in balance.* That's what's meant by the term *natural body weight*—it comes easily, comfortably, from a process of eating, exercising, and engaging in a lifestyle that's healthy and right for you.

You can't impose a weight on your body and expect to maintain it, any more than you can impose a diet on your appetite and expect to eat that way forever. Although you have similar genetics, you may not have the same body type as your mother, father, sister or brother. Even though you may be the same height as a friend or colleague, you have a different shape, body build, and bone structure. You have a unique metabolism that's yours and yours alone. Each of these factors will impact what weight is natural for your body at your age.

Learning to trust your body is like learning to trust your feelings. It takes time and you can't rush the process.

How about setting a goal to let your body decide where it wants to settle and giving yourself time to get there? That means not weighing yourself or using an old pair of size 6s as a marker to judge if you've lost or gained weight. I understand that this is a lot to ask, especially when you've been a disordered eater for some or all of your life. Maybe you can't even imagine trusting the body you believe has betrayed you by abusing food for so long. Think about it, though: is it really your body that's been untrustworthy or the way you've been caring for it? Learning to trust your body is like learning to trust your feelings. It takes time and you can't rush the process.

Before you close this book, I'd like you to do one more *Stop and Feel* exercise. Take a minute (yes, this minute right now) and notice your breathing. Draw a few deep breaths until your mind slows down. Close your eyes, clear your mind, and ask yourself what you are feeling. Let your emotions float up to the surface without judgment and just see what happens.

Are you a little excited that you've found a new way to deal with your food problems? Somewhat doubtful that the process really works? Sit with whatever you're experiencing for as long as it's there and don't feel compelled to do anything about it. Tell yourself that if the emotion stays, fine; if not, okay too. Notice if you're having any feelings *about* your feelings, especially judgments. *Let them go as well by finding a place in your heart that's interested in why you feel as you do, and replace your judgments with curiosity and compassion.* Gently open your heart to wondering about your tendency to be critical and hard on yourself. Is it time to let go of the critic? Notice any stirrings about wanting to treat yourself better—being kinder to yourself, less harsh, and more reflective, patient, realistic, aware, and forgiving.

When you're satisfied that you know how you feel about the material in this book, it's time to move on. More feelings will arise, maybe the same ones you just felt, or different ones. Maybe a whole mix of them. It doesn't matter. You don't have to feel a certain way about what you've read, about your eating, your body, or anything else. Your work for now is only to experience and know exactly what you feel *in this very moment*. If you've figured that out, you're on your way.

FURTHER EXPLORATION

1. What are your feelings about finishing this book?

2. What are you feeling about giving up acting out with food?

3. Are you more concerned with giving up a food obsession, feeling painful emotions, or gaining or losing weight?

4. What are three ways you intend to change your relationship with food?

5. What would it feel like to maintain a comfortable, natural, healthy weight through "normal" eating?

6. What would it feel like to give up your quest for a specific weight, that is, what would change in your life for the better or for the worse?

____

____

____

7. What other significant problems in your life have you been avoiding by focusing on food and weight?

____

____

____

8. What are five things you're going to do differently today to stay in touch with your feelings and not obsess about food and weight?

____

____

____

9. What are five more things you're going to do differently this week to stay in touch with your feelings and not obsess about food and weight?

____

____

____

10. What are five more things you're going to do differently this year to stay in touch with your feelings and not obsess about food and weight?

____

____

____

Food & Feelings Post-Assessment

Now that you've arrived at the end of this book, it's time to take the *Food & Feelings Post-Assessment* to discover what you've learned, how you've changed, and what specific areas you still need to work on to do a top-notch job of handling both food and feelings. As with the *Pre-Assessment*, please give each statement some thought before responding, be honest, and try not to make judgments. No peeking at the *Pre-Assessment* either. After you've completed the *Post-Assessment*, you'll be ready for comparison and discovery.

Once again, pay attention to feelings that arise by jotting them down, but don't get too caught up in experiencing them until you've completed the assessment. When you're done, return to the *Pre-Assessment* and compare your responses. First, without focusing on specific responses, note where they fall (low, mid or high numbers) and get a sense of movement. Second, carefully go over the assessment and focus on the change or lack of change in each answer. If you'd hoped for more improvement, remember not to be judgmental; remain curious and compassionate. Focus on the changes you have made and try to stay positive and hopeful. Third, use the *Food & Feelings Action Plan* on page 213 to summarize your progress and help you make future changes.

Instructions: Circle the number that best describes your response to each statement. The number 1 represents *least* or *least often* and the number 10 represents *most* or *most often*. Note that in both assessments the words feelings and emotions are used interchangeably.

FEELINGS

	(least)									(most)
1. I am in touch with my feelings.	1	2	3	4	5	6	7	8	9	10
2. I can generally identify and label what I'm feeling.	1	2	3	4	5	6	7	8	9	10
3. I am accepting of all of my feelings.	1	2	3	4	5	6	7	8	9	10
4. I am willing to experience all of my feelings.	1	2	3	4	5	6	7	8	9	10
5. I understand the purpose of feelings.	1	2	3	4	5	6	7	8	9	10
6. I value all of my feelings.	1	2	3	4	5	6	7	8	9	10

7. I give equal weight to all of my feelings.	1 2 3 4 5 6 7 8 9 10
8. I listen to what my feelings have to tell me.	1 2 3 4 5 6 7 8 9 10
9. I don't judge my feelings.	1 2 3 4 5 6 7 8 9 10
10. I reflect on and try to understand my feelings.	1 2 3 4 5 6 7 8 9 10
11. I am curious about my feelings.	1 2 3 4 5 6 7 8 9 10
12. I believe all feelings are bearable.	1 2 3 4 5 6 7 8 9 10
13. I trust my emotions to help guide my life.	1 2 3 4 5 6 7 8 9 10
14. I am effective at taking care of myself when I'm upset.	1 2 3 4 5 6 7 8 9 10
15. I express my feelings appropriately.	1 2 3 4 5 6 7 8 9 10
16. I can tolerate intense feelings well.	1 2 3 4 5 6 7 8 9 10
17. I don't act out my feelings.	1 2 3 4 5 6 7 8 9 10
18. I have healthy, rational beliefs about feelings.	1 2 3 4 5 6 7 8 9 10
19. I don't let other people tell me what to feel.	1 2 3 4 5 6 7 8 9 10
20. I understand the meaning of projection.	1 2 3 4 5 6 7 8 9 10
21. I understand what defense mechanisms are.	1 2 3 4 5 6 7 8 9 10
22. I understand what transference reaction means.	1 2 3 4 5 6 7 8 9 10
23. I understand what secondary emotions are.	1 2 3 4 5 6 7 8 9 10
24. I can distinguish voluntary from involuntary suffering.	1 2 3 4 5 6 7 8 9 10
25. I don't experience much voluntary suffering in my life.	1 2 3 4 5 6 7 8 9 10
26. I know what signal anxiety is.	1 2 3 4 5 6 7 8 9 10
27. I know that people can't make me feel emotions.	1 2 3 4 5 6 7 8 9 10
28. I know when I'm feeling guilty.	1 2 3 4 5 6 7 8 9 10
29. I feel guilty only when it's appropriate.	1 2 3 4 5 6 7 8 9 10
30. I don't let other people guilt-trip me.	1 2 3 4 5 6 7 8 9 10
31. I handle feeling guilty effectively.	1 2 3 4 5 6 7 8 9 10
32. I express my guilt appropriately.	1 2 3 4 5 6 7 8 9 10
33. I understand the purpose of guilt.	1 2 3 4 5 6 7 8 9 10
34. I know when I'm feeling ashamed.	1 2 3 4 5 6 7 8 9 10
35. I can distinguish guilt from shame.	1 2 3 4 5 6 7 8 9 10
36. I can distinguish shame from embarrassment.	1 2 3 4 5 6 7 8 9 10
37. I feel ashamed only when it's appropriate.	1 2 3 4 5 6 7 8 9 10
38. I know people can't make me feel ashamed.	1 2 3 4 5 6 7 8 9 10
39. I handle feeling ashamed effectively.	1 2 3 4 5 6 7 8 9 10
40. I express my shame appropriately.	1 2 3 4 5 6 7 8 9 10
41. I understand the purpose of shame.	1 2 3 4 5 6 7 8 9 10
42. I know when I'm feeling helpless.	1 2 3 4 5 6 7 8 9 10
43. I accept that I can't avoid feeling helpless sometimes.	1 2 3 4 5 6 7 8 9 10
44. I handle feeling helpless effectively.	1 2 3 4 5 6 7 8 9 10
45. I express helplessness appropriately.	1 2 3 4 5 6 7 8 9 10
46. I understand the purpose of helplessness.	1 2 3 4 5 6 7 8 9 10
47. I know when I'm feeling anxious.	1 2 3 4 5 6 7 8 9 10
48. I understand the purpose of anxiety.	1 2 3 4 5 6 7 8 9 10

49. I handle feeling anxious effectively.	1	2	3	4	5	6	7	8	9	10
50. I express my anxiety appropriately.	1	2	3	4	5	6	7	8	9	10
51. I don't have much signal anxiety.	1	2	3	4	5	6	7	8	9	10
52. I know when I'm feeling disappointed.	1	2	3	4	5	6	7	8	9	10
53. I understand the purpose of disappointment.	1	2	3	4	5	6	7	8	9	10
54. I handle disappointment effectively.	1	2	3	4	5	6	7	8	9	10
55. I express disappointment appropriately.	1	2	3	4	5	6	7	8	9	10
56. I learn from disappointment.	1	2	3	4	5	6	7	8	9	10
57. I know when I'm confused.	1	2	3	4	5	6	7	8	9	10
58. I can distinguish confusion from mixed feelings.	1	2	3	4	5	6	7	8	9	10
59. I understand why people become confused.	1	2	3	4	5	6	7	8	9	10
60. I handle being confused effectively.	1	2	3	4	5	6	7	8	9	10
61. I express my confusion appropriately.	1	2	3	4	5	6	7	8	9	10
62. I know when I have conflicted or mixed feelings.	1	2	3	4	5	6	7	8	9	10
63. I understand the necessity of conflicted feelings.	1	2	3	4	5	6	7	8	9	10
64. I tolerate having mixed feelings well.	1	2	3	4	5	6	7	8	9	10
65. I express feeling conflicted appropriately.	1	2	3	4	5	6	7	8	9	10
66. I know when I'm feeling lonely.	1	2	3	4	5	6	7	8	9	10
67. I understand the purpose of loneliness.	1	2	3	4	5	6	7	8	9	10
68. I handle loneliness effectively.	1	2	3	4	5	6	7	8	9	10
69. I express feeling lonely appropriately.	1	2	3	4	5	6	7	8	9	10

FOOD

70. I can distinguish emotional from physical hunger.	1	2	3	4	5	6	7	8	9	10
71. I experience feelings rather than focus on food/weight.	1	2	3	4	5	6	7	8	9	10
72. I allow myself to feel guilty, not focus on food/weight.	1	2	3	4	5	6	7	8	9	10
73. I allow myself to feel shame, not focus on food/weight.	1	2	3	4	5	6	7	8	9	10
74. I allow myself to feel helpless, not focus on food/weight.	1	2	3	4	5	6	7	8	9	10
75. I allow myself to feel anxious, not focus on food/weight.	1	2	3	4	5	6	7	8	9	10
76. I allow myself to feel disappointed, not focus on food/weight.	1	2	3	4	5	6	7	8	9	10
77. I allow myself to feel confused or conflicted, not focus on food/weight.	1	2	3	4	5	6	7	8	9	10
78. I allow myself to feel lonely, not focus on food/weight.	1	2	3	4	5	6	7	8	9	10
79. I express feelings appropriately without using food.	1	2	3	4	5	6	7	8	9	10
80. I accept that "normal" eaters occasionally use food when they're upset.	1	2	3	4	5	6	7	8	9	10
81. I'm compassionate with myself when I use food inappropriately.	1	2	3	4	5	6	7	8	9	10
82. I turn to people, not a food/weight focus when I'm upset.	1	2	3	4	5	6	7	8	9	10
83. I trust myself not to focus on food/weight when I'm upset.	1	2	3	4	5	6	7	8	9	10
84. My life is emotionally full and satisfying.	1	2	3	4	5	6	7	8	9	10
85. I know food won't make me feel better when I'm upset.	1	2	3	4	5	6	7	8	9	10
86. I try hard not to focus on food when I'm upset.	1	2	3	4	5	6	7	8	9	10
87. If I eat when I'm upset, I can usually stop myself.	1	2	3	4	5	6	7	8	9	10

88. I get my emotional needs met without using food. 1 2 3 4 5 6 7 8 9 10
89. I'm gentle with myself if I use food when I'm upset. 1 2 3 4 5 6 7 8 9 10
90. I listen to whether my body wants to eat or not eat when I'm upset, and either is okay. 1 2 3 4 5 6 7 8 9 10
91. I value nourishing myself with food even when I'm upset. 1 2 3 4 5 6 7 8 9 10
92. I want to be emotionally healthy more than I want to distract myself. 1 2 3 4 5 6 7 8 9 10
93. I'm hopeful that I'll overcome my disordered eating. 1 2 3 4 5 6 7 8 9 10
94. I know that I won't end my disordered eating overnight. 1 2 3 4 5 6 7 8 9 10
95. I acknowledge that to end disordered eating I may need help from a therapist. 1 2 3 4 5 6 7 8 9 10
96. I acknowledge that to end disordered eating I may need to join an eating disorder support group. 1 2 3 4 5 6 7 8 9 10
97. I am aware that unless I'm emotionally healthy, I may end disordered eating and adopt other unhealthy behaviors. 1 2 3 4 5 6 7 8 9 10
98. I can visualize myself being emotionally healthy and a "normal" eater. 1 2 3 4 5 6 7 8 9 10
99. I can visualize being comfortable in my body whether or not my weight "changes when I'm eating "normally." 1 2 3 4 5 6 7 8 9 10
100. I am committed to becoming emotionally healthy and recovering from disordered eating. 1 2 3 4 5 6 7 8 9 10

Food & Feelings Action Plan

This worksheet summarizes the changes you've made by comparing your responses from the *Pre-* and *Post-Assessments*. It should be completed right after you finish the *Post Assessment*. At a glance, it tells you the food and feeling areas in which you've made attitudinal and behavioral progress and those which still need work. Continue to review this plan from time to time to reflect on your progress.

Instructions: Write a word or phrase that describes an attitude or a behavior such as "don't eat when hungry" or "judge self after binge" under the column that best describes your progress or lack thereof. Use this assessment scale.

- Complete Change – a 180-degree turnaround
- Substantial Change = a major breakthrough but aren't quite where you want to be
- Some Change = minimal change
- No Change = your behavior or attitude hasn't budged
- Needs Work = areas you wish to continue to work on, whether to get unstuck or improve performance

Complete Change	**Substantial Change**	**Some Change**	**No Change**	**Needs Work**

Complete Change	Substantial Change	Some Change	No Change	Needs Work

About the Author

Karen R. Koenig, LCSW, M.Ed., is a psychotherapist, educator, and expert on the psychology of eating who has over 25 years experience treating people with food and weight issues. Author of the widely-used book, *The Rules of "Normal" Eating*, she helps people become "normal" eaters through her therapy practice and workshops. She has written numerous articles on clinical issues for both local and national publications, and is an experienced, dynamic public speaker. She lives with her husband in Sarasota, FL. Visit her website at *www.eatingnormal.com.*

About the Publisher

Since 1980, Gürze Books has been dedicated to providing quality information on eating disorders recovery, research, education, advocacy, and prevention. They publish *Eating Disorders Today*, a newsletter for individuals in recovery and their loved ones and the *Eating Disorders Review*, a clinical newsletter for professionals. The company also widely distributes the *Eating Disorders Resource Catalogue*, and hosts two helpful websites, *www.gurze.com* and *www.eatingdisordersblogs.com*.

Order at www.gurze.com
Or by phone 800/756-7533

The Food & Feelings Workbook is available at bookstores and libraries and may be ordered directly from the Gürze Books website, *www.gurze.com*, or by phone 800/756-7533.

FREE Catalogue

The Eating Disorders Resource Catalogue features books on eating and weight-related topics, including body image, size acceptance, self-esteem and more. It also includes listings of nonprofit associations and treatment facilities and is handed out by therapists, educators, and other health care professionals around the world.

Eating Disorders Today

This compassionate and supportive newsletter for individuals in recovery and their loved ones combines helpful facts and self-help advice from experts in the field of eating disorders. Quarterly subscriptions available. Request a sample issue.

www.gurze.com

Visit our website for additional resources, including many free articles, hundreds of books, and links to organizations, treatment facilities and other websites.

www.eatingdisordersblogs.com

EatingDisordersBlogs.com is a website with author blogs for connecting with others about food and feelings, healthy eating, family concerns, and recovery issues.

Gürze Books has specialized in eating disorders publications and education since 1980.